10 Little Rules
for
Navigating Change

Stories of Resilience, Leadership and Growth

by Women in Geospatial Leadership

compiled and edited by Carol Pearson

Books in the 10 Little Rules Series

10 Little Rules for a Blissy Life by Carol Pearson

10 Little Rules for Your Creative Soul by Rita Long

10 Little Rules of Hank by Wendy Price

10 Little Rules for Finding Your Truth by Micki Beach

10 Little Rules for Mermaids by Amy Hege Atwell

10 Little Rules for the Modern Southern Belle by Beverly Ingle

10 Little Rules for Serving You by Amy Hege Atwell

10 Little Rules for Sharing Your Story by Frank Winters

10 Little Rules When Good Jobs Go Bad by Kathleen Goggin

10 Little Rules for a Double-Butted Adventure by Teri M Brown

10 Little Rules for Understanding America by Danny Zimny-Schmitt

10 Little Rules for Getting IT Done by Jenn Lorenz

10 Little Rules for Navigating Change
by Women in Geospatial Leadership
compiled and edited by Carol Pearson

DEDICATION

To all current and future leaders—may we continue to navigate change with courage, curiosity and care, helping to make the world a better place.

The authors of "10 Little Rules for Navigating Change" have chosen to donate 100% of their royalties from the sale of this book to the National Geospatial Collaborative (NGC). By purchasing this book, you are amplifying NGC's mission to boldly pursue a more effective geospatial ecosystem.

Learn more at nationalgeospatialcollaborative.org

CONTENTS

Preface 13

Rule 1 ~ Say It Out Loud *by Jenna Leveille* 19

Rule 2 ~ Use the Right Tool *by Angela Witcher* 35

Rule 3 ~ Find Your Allies *by Shea Lemar* 53

Rule 4 ~ Mobilize Your Village *by Megan Compton* 67

Rule 5 ~ Prioritize, then Adapt *by Erin Fashoway* 89

Rule 6 ~ Embrace the Imperfect *by Natalie Lee* 107

Rule 7 ~ Walk Through the Door Anyway *by Susan Miller* 131

Rule 8 ~ Embrace the Uncertainty *by Kate Hickey* 151

Rule 9 ~ Be Uniquely You *by Lindsey Peña PhD* 167

Rule 10 ~ Find Your Joy *by Karen Rogers* 187

Acknowledgements 199

End Notes 200

Your turn, your rules 202

PREFACE

The idea of collaborating on a book sprouted as the outcome of a breakfast meeting. Twice a year, geospatial technology leaders across sectors gather to exchange ideas, collaborate, celebrate, and problem-solve at meetings hosted by the National States Geographic Information Council (NSGIC). The NSGIC GeoWomen in Leadership Workgroup meeting is a staple of each event. Organized and facilitated by the NSGIC GeoWomen Co-chairs, each gathering has a topic theme and typically follows a discussion-focused format. While the purpose of the Workgroup is to support and promote women in geospatial leadership positions, the biannual meetings are for everyone; the discussion topics tend to be professional development oriented and are equally relevant to any gender and career stage. Attendance and engagement runs high for these early morning discussions. The energy and commitment from this community to each other is evident in their participation amid a busy and demanding conference schedule with enlightening networking.

In late 2024, as the GeoWomen Co-chairs prepared for the February 2025 NSGIC Midyear Meeting, our discussions centered on navigating change. That year had been particularly challenging for many of us, our colleagues, our families and friends, both professionally and personally. Looking forward to 2025, the group collectively held our breath in anticipation of administration changes at both federal and state levels. Several members of our Co-chair group had already experienced major life changes in 2024 and more were anticipated.

Strategies for navigating through these experiences became our theme and our hope; to provide a space to lean in to change and discover tools for resilience and growth as a community. It worked! We could not have predicted a more honest, vulnerable, and productive discussion.

As professionals and as people, we've lived through extraordinary transitions in recent years. The early years of this decade have tested all of us—through a global pandemic, shifting priorities in our workplaces, and a world that seems to change faster each day. From the disruption of COVID-19 to changes in leadership at every level of government, our professional and personal worlds have been reshaped in ways few could have anticipated.

Regardless of where one stands politically, by the time we came together for the 2025 Midyear Meeting, the transitions and policies of the second Trump administration had brought significant shifts across federal and state agencies—creating both uncertainty and opportunity, and leaving many of us navigating unfamiliar territory in our work and our personal lives. And while the United States may feel deeply divided— and we as its citizens may not always agree on the causes or outcomes of change—we all face the same question: How do we navigate it?

Our hope, and our shared commitment, is to do so with dignity, empathy, and purpose.

Wednesday morning of the Midyear meeting conference attendees gathered for the GeoWomen breakfast. As we took our seats at round tables for 10, the topic of change was introduced and a series of questions were discussed at each of the tables. The responses were reported out for discussion with the larger group. What followed was personal, insightful and emotional—strategies for dealing with grief after losing a loved one, finding joy when facing challenges you can't change, becoming comfortable with uncertainty, and so many more.

After the session, women from our table looked at the notes taken and reflected out loud, "these would be a great 10 Little Rules book!" Many of us had just been exposed to our first 10 Little Rules book—"10 Little Rules for Sharing Your Story" by Frank Winters, one of NSGIC's leaders and a friend to most everyone at NSGIC. And so it was that a few months later, we gathered to discuss the possibility of writing a book together! And we did!

The authors of this book are friends, colleagues, and co-conspirators; some are NSGIC GeoWomen in Leadership Workgroup Co-chairs, and all are women passionate about geospatial solutions, leadership, and supporting and promoting diversity and each other. We are as diverse as our contributions. State, federal, industry, and non-profit leaders, we hail from different states, with different backgrounds and origin stories; we are single, married, and divorced; we are girlfriends, wives, moms, sisters, daughters, and caregivers; we are adventurous and solitary, brave and vulnerable, introverts and extroverts. We are all, in some flavor, what we imagine our readers to be.

As we discussed our book, images of water and navigating continued to surface. As geographers, we often find ourselves visualizing our processes and plans with metaphors and maps. In our lives, we are charting a course along uncertain waters; some quiet and peaceful, others exciting and exhilarating; still others full of fear and uncertainty. As we encounter obstacles—the turbulent rapids of conflict and difficult life experiences — the guides, maps, lessons and lived experiences of our past, our friends, and those we encounter help us navigate. Once in quieter waters, we share those lessons, a value we all hold dear and bring to our friendships and colleagues, and now, to you.

Writing this book and sharing our stories is scary and exciting for each of us in our own way—it is uncharted territory. We are grateful to have you with us and hope you learn, grow, and find your own strategies for navigating change. Enjoy!

Jenna, Angela, Shea, Megan, Erin, Natalie, Susan, Kate, Lindsey and Karen

RULE 1
Say It Out Loud
by Jenna Leveille

Voicing the things that are worrying or causing anxiety is a technique my husband and I use regularly. We have found that it helps us avoid conflict, increases our opportunity for connection, builds trust and, most importantly, reduces my husband's anxious tendencies. It is worth saying (out loud) that our human attachment to our internal dialog—which includes all our fears, doubts and assumptions—too often makes this challenging to put into practice. I would argue that it is worth the effort, every time.

My husband Phillip is one of those people everyone likes. He is funny and gregarious, kind and thoughtful, and genuinely cares about people he has never met. He is the best human I have ever known. His contagious smile and laughter, thoughtful nature and genuine desire to make the world a better place are a consistent inspiration and only a few of the many reasons he had my heart at hello. When he met my mom for the first time, she declared he had the "happy gene" everyone desired. He is a light in the world. Ironically, being a light for others does not always translate to being a light for ourselves.

Humans struggle. We can all relate. Our paths are rarely linear and are never free of change, challenge and opportunities for growth—both externally and internally. Sometimes unexpected events upend our perceptions of ourselves, our relationships and how we encounter the world. Eighteen months into our marriage, on Christmas Eve, Phillip was admitted to the hospital. His heart rate, at over 180 bpm, brought us to the emergency room. After nearly seven hours, the medical staff were finally able to slow his racing heart. We spent Christmas (sans Charlie Brown tree and presents) in the hospital and by New Years, we were home with little understanding of what had caused the episode. Phillip was shaken and vulnerable in a new and unexpected way, and didn't know how to articulate what he was thinking or feeling. It is worth sharing that just prior to his struggles with his heart, Phillip made the difficult choice to leave a toxic work environment and reinvent himself. He bravely returned to college midlife and embarked on a new career path in an industry he had passion for but no prior experience in.

Over the following months we learned he had experienced atrial flutter, a condition in which the nerves in his heart would misfire and cause a cascade of symptoms and discomfort. Atrial flutter is a known condition with a known solution and fortunately, in our modern medical age, is curable. Surgery is required but it is a comparatively simple and safe procedure. It is still heart surgery.

The following March (coincidentally the weekend prior to the world shutting down due to COVID), Phillip went in for what we expected to be a standard outpatient ablation procedure. In his case, he was the unicorn, and the procedure was not standard. Gratefully, the procedure was a success but, due to surgical complications, Phillip was once again admitted to the hospital, this time with COVID looming. It is only in hindsight that we were able to see the small but significant stressors that occurred throughout the few months of uncertainty prior to surgery. The day he was discharged, quarantine began.

Phillip is an extrovert. My introvert sister once described the difference between an introvert and an extrovert daily experience this way: each day an introvert wakes with a standard allotment of cookies. As the day progresses, with each interaction the introvert gives their cookies away and by the end of the day they have no more cookies and are exhausted from the exchanges. An extrovert, on the other hand, wakes each day without cookies. They go out into the world seeking cookies and by the end of a good day, they are full of cookies and energized, ready to tackle any challenge and feel fulfilled. It is a great analogy that resonates for me.

During COVID, Phillip woke each day without cookies and struggled to find a solution to fill the void he felt. Quarantine was difficult for everyone—except perhaps for extreme introverts. Post heart surgery he was left feeling anxious, vulnerable and very isolated. Coping was challenging and the presiding COVID climate was fearful, uncertain and frustrating, further reinforcing his inner dialog and feelings of mortality.

We survived COVID isolation comparatively well. Unlike so many others, COVID had minimal impact on our world, family and friends. We were acutely aware of and grateful for our good health, but cautious when quarantine ended. What went unsaid was the toll the isolation, coupled with heart trauma, took on Phillip.

As the world slowly came out of quarantine, we worked to find balance and restore our social and physical selves. Phillip was still struggling but externally seemed to turn a corner and was once again engaged in the world and his new career path. He took a chance at what he deemed a "dream job," even though he didn't have the required educational background or experience. The risk paid off and he was hired.

On a winter day of the same year, he woke up feeling like he had pulled a muscle in his back. We both dismissed his feeling as "normal" for our middle-aged life. Within a week he had lost the use of his right hand, then in time his arm, and was experiencing constant excruciating pain. As the days and then weeks went by, he was unable to sleep for more than minutes at a time; relief was an unattainable wish. I was desperate to help and completely at a loss as to how.

Eventually, we found a neurosurgeon who identified the compression of nerves in his neck. Phillip would need surgery but would heal. After the surgery (fusion of his cervical spine), he finally experienced relief and regained the use of his right arm. We were both optimistic about his recovery and exhausted. He was supported throughout by his new employer and while still anxious, felt hopeful. Four days after the surgery, he lost feeling in his left arm.

We soon learned he had experienced a rare complication from the surgery—C5 palsy. It would take time but he would recover fully. In the meantime, Phillip had limited function on his left side, which would take months to heal and many more months of intense physical therapy to regain his strength and full function.

His mental, emotional and physical well being had taken a devastating blow.

It took more than a year for Phillip to feel physically recovered. He is still working on his mental and emotional well-being and continues to make strides. He will easily admit that the trauma he experienced fundamentally changed him.

Throughout the years of this part of our journey together, we struggled to comfort and understand each other; to maintain "us" with all that was happening and beyond our control. Our experiences were different and yet had some profound similarities. We were both isolated and inseparable. The natural tension from the dichotomy of our emotions was oddly motivating. Discomfort, we grew to learn, is not always something that should or can be avoided. Often, it is an opportunity for growth.

It brings me comfort to know that humans are resilient and adaptable. I believe we always and inevitably find our way; some with more ease than others. Like many couples, our love for and commitment to each other has kept us together. We are problem solvers. We have sought help, been both patient and impatient with our process, raged and cried at and with each other, and still continue to develop strategies to do better. Some days it truly feels like we have tried every solution, comfort and approach with varying success;

other days we feel the optimism that comes with a new day and a chance at discovering a fresh perspective.

Phillip and I have always had just one house rule: If you don't like something, do something about it (complaining is not doing). Our adherence to this rule has prevented countless petty fights, resentment and misunderstandings and works well for the day to day care of our house and each other. Recently, we have adopted another rule. Though we have yet to declare it our "official" second rule, saying things out loud is a tremendous help for both of us.

Take a moment and give some thought to your inner dialog, especially the scary or worrisome things you can't shake. Try saying the things that flow through your mind out loud so you can hear them with a different part of your brain; ideally the curious part. Frank Winters, a dear friend and fellow 10 Little Rules author, noted in his book "10 Little Rules for Sharing Your Story" (Winters, 2024) that it is impossible to be curious and experience fight or flight (or be anxious) at the same time. (If you haven't read his book, it is worth your time; I highly recommend it.)

I have practiced this both alone and with Phillip. When I do, I am able to find a fresh perspective that allows my feelings, whatever they are, to change; things that scare me are put in proportion and I find myself less afraid or not afraid at all. Being able to identify the things I am unable to change and let them go prevents those repetitive worried thoughts that all too easily spiral internally. By saying the scary parts out loud, and listening to myself speak them with curiosity, I am able to deliberately choose where I put my thoughts and energy.

For Phillip, the same technique has given him a tool to quiet his racing mind, recognize his well being and health, and let go of the sometimes overwhelming anxiety he experiences. Together, we are better equipped to care for each other, thoughtfully provide comfort or a solution depending on what the other needs, and most importantly understand we are not alone.

Sometimes the most profound tools are those that appear simple and easy to practice. This rule is like this for me. It seems simple, yet in practice I know it's often hard to say these scary things out loud.

I believe the things that go unspoken are the very things that we need to say.

About the Author

Jenna Leveille is Vice President of State and Local Government at the Sanborn Map Company, with over 25 years of experience in GIS. A graduate of Oregon State University, she has led strategic geospatial initiatives across government, including serving as Arizona's Deputy State Cartographer (2017–2024). At Sanborn, Jenna guides geospatial strategy and supports state and local governments in planning, coordination, and data development. She is a passionate advocate for servant leadership, data-driven decision-making, workforce development, and inclusion. Jenna volunteers with the National Geospatial Collaborative and NSGIC, and enjoys photography, quilting, and outdoor adventures with her husband and puppy.

your turn...

Say it out loud

What scary or troubling thoughts have crept into your inner dialogue lately? Do you find any particular worries repeating themselves?

Pick one thought, take a deep breath, and say it out loud. How did that feel?

Now, take another breath and, with a spirit of curiosity, say it again and really listen to yourself speaking. Did it feel different this time? Does it seem maybe a little more manageable?

How might it feel different if you said the scary parts out loud to someone else in your life?

Use the journaling space on the next few pages to write down your thoughts.

_____

_____

_____

_____

_____

_____

_____

_____

_____

_____

_____

_____

_____

_____

_____

Women in Geospatial Leadership

RULE 2
Use the Right Tool
by Angela Witcher

Life begins with change. We navigate change from the moment we come out of the womb, leaving warmth and familiarity for a bright, strange, and colder experience. Still next to mother, but now she has changed too.

We will all be adapting to change for the rest of our lives. It is challenging, no doubt, but I've always found these words from poet Edwin Markham inspirational:

For all your days prepare,
And meet them ever alike:
When you are the anvil bear –
When you are the hammer, strike.
Preparedness, Edwin Markham, 1919

Like the anvil upon which iron workers execute their craft, you will have to bear changes, sometimes hard changes. So be prepared to take the blows. You must be the anvil when ...

... change is inevitable. Your kids will grow up. Let them.

... change is wrong. Don't sign that contract if the situation doesn't feel right.

... change is not well thought out. Move slowly; another change is probably coming.

... change is confusing. Observe and evaluate. Go into change cautiously.

... it's somebody else's turn. Be mature and be gracious.

... when the reward is in the future. This is the easiest way to bear change. Be patient.

Sometimes you'll be the hammer, prepared to strike in order to build or break as necessary. This is how you grow and reinvent yourself, your family, and your community with intention. Be the hammer when ...

... you know change is right. When you have the hammer and you can make things better, do it.

... you can save someone. Not everyone has a hammer, and no one has the hammer all the time. Use it for good and save someone when you can.

... you have to be authentically you to change other people's perception of who you are to change your situation. Yes, it may make them uncomfortable. Regardless, be who you are, not who they think you are or who they want you to be.

Markham tells us how to prepare, to be ready to be the anvil or the hammer depending on the situation. Yet we need to develop the wisdom to navigate change successfully. Without wisdom, neither the anvil nor the hammer will do us any good. We obtain this wisdom from observation, thoughtfulness, and experience. The wisdom helps you manage change, and helps you learn from the change you experience.

My wisdom was gained from myriad experiences. I grew up in rural New Jersey, the Garden State, and we had the biggest garden in our community. My father planted it, my mother cooked from it, and I planted on cold spring mornings, pulled weeds, shelled peas and snapped beans to prepare for Sunday dinner.

We also had a wood lot behind our house. Playing in the woods was one of my favorite pastimes. Taking walks down the trail, sitting on a fallen tree, running from spiders, and feeling that sense of awe when the trail opened up to a beautiful field; these are some of my best childhood memories. The experience was even sweeter because I had friends to share it with and no cell phones to distract us.

This region in Central Jersey is known as the Sourland Mountains (geologically it is a ridge). It was slow to develop because the rocky soil did not make for good wells or septic. Prime farmland was developed first, so the Sourlands remained untouched until the advent of modern engineering. As I was growing up, I knew everyone didn't have this lifestyle, but I had no idea how much change was coming.

As a young GIS professional, I used to host GIS Day for students at my agency. At one point I created an exercise to visualize land use changes. A picture is worth a thousand words, and GIS is fluent. So at the end of the exercise, I was ready for a vigorous conversation on the loss of agriculture and forestry, and growth of urbanization in our state. Yet my exercise did not have the impact I had imagined. Many of the students didn't see my point about the growing loss of natural areas. Even if they did, they were not disturbed. I realized they had not grown up playing in the woods, so they had no personal stake in the change. As change happens around you, people change around you. When you stop and think, you suddenly notice that the world has changed.

Despite all the jokes about New Jersey, people can't stop coming here. Sitting between New York City and Philadelphia, with a substantial coastline plus good schools and universities, there is a lot that attracts people to this little state. Yet just like a horse who loves to graze on grass but stamps it out in the corral with too many footsteps, too many people ruin the features they came to New Jersey to enjoy.

Environmentalists were my first example of how all change doesn't need to be accepted. One does not have to accept someone else's vision of what your neighborhood should look like. Yes, change is inevitable, yet sometimes you can pick up that hammer and help define that change, blunt the effects of unwanted change, or steer the change in a different direction.

Change has been managed very well where I live. It is zoned for Mountain Resource Conservation; there is a 14 acre minimum to build a new house. Best of all, there are no plans for running sewer lines into the region, which are the forerunners of urbanization. Advocacy and geology (two effective "hammers") came together to protect this special place. I guess that rocky soil is good for something after all.

Environmentalists know that landscape changes impact how we perceive the world. As a young adult I observed my father resisting huge changes when a developer cut down the 100-year-old trees lining the entrance to our historical cemetery that dates back to the 1850s. Those trees were planted by our ancestors. The developer cleared land to squeeze in as many houses as possible, resulting in brand new homes erected uncomfortably close to old headstones. It was devastating to see this massive change.

At one point a barricade was placed across the cemetery driveway to block our entry. It appeared our cemetery was destined to the fate of so many historical African American burial grounds: to have markers destroyed, graves built over, and people forgotten. While the developer was busy creating his vision, my father was busier. He refused to be the anvil, bending to the developer's will. So he picked up his hammer. He sent messages to all the descendants that he knew, hosted meetings to keep everyone informed of what was happening, raised money, lobbied local politicians, and retained a well-established law firm.

A new survey was commissioned, and a grant acquired to install fencing to demarcate the property line. Eventually, quiet title was obtained, and the cemetery was officially under the stewardship of the newly established Pennington African Cemetery Association. Dad was elected President and appeared in several newspaper articles and received additional grants and even proclamations from a state senator when he passed. He saw the change coming, and he took action. He did not have as much money as the developer, and there is no profit in maintaining a cemetery. But he knew the people buried there—the United States Colored Troops who volunteered to fight in the Civil War, his grandparents, an uncle, a teenage friend for whom he served as a pall bearer, and more. Fighting change can be hard emotionally and financially, but when it is a matter of family and legacy, there is no other option. You must commit to your path and muscle through.

I wish I could say the story of the cemetery ended there, and we all lived happily ever after. Unfortunately, that's not true, but the example of pride, intelligence and determination shown by the founding members of the Pennington African Cemetery Association continues to empower their successors as we face change in our generation.

For survival, mankind has learned to be resilient, to adapt. Some people, especially women, are taught to manage whatever comes our way, rather than actively choosing what we want. Fortunately I've seen that changing over my lifetime. Everyone needs the skills to be both the anvil and the hammer. We must know when to be resilient, and when to be the change agent.

Choosing Change

I had been a GIS Specialist for 15 years when I experienced a major change. I worked on data development projects, led a training program, and served on conference committees. Even though I was working in GIS and liked the people I was working with, something was missing in my heart. I felt stuck—and that impacted my thinking. If you had asked me if I was qualified to do anything else, I would have told you "No."

Then an opportunity presented itself. My chain of command changed, and I heard rumblings through the grapevine of new opportunities. I updated my resume and watched for possible opportunities. Then it came: Project managers were needed to manage some multi-year grants. It was a thrilling idea, yet felt fraught with risk. I was a GIS professional, and this was not GIS. It would be new work, new responsibilities, new colleagues, and no new money. I had good reasons to stay in my role, yet I was prepared to be the hammer and leapt at the opportunity.

My heart was filled, even while the change was rough. I had to learn different technologies, new communication styles, and the new normal of long hours at the office. There was so much work to keep up with that at times the frustration was overwhelming. Still, I never wanted to go back to my old job. I knew I was where I was supposed to be. As time went on, I had to navigate more changes at work with increased responsibilities at home. Quitting was never an option. The only direction to go was forward, so I committed to my path and muscled through.

Tips for Managing Change

Change can be good, bad, and often both at the same time, and life never stops changing. What I've learned along the way is the importance of working hard and always being your authentic self. This is the key to give you inner peace and put you in the best position to navigate change.

Stay healthy

- Anxiety can throw off eating and sleeping habits. Pay attention to this and take care of yourself, to retain your strength and focus.

- Find people who affirm your self-worth, but not necessarily your opinion. You need respectful and intelligent input to make decisions. Stay centered in the rocking boat of change. Roll with it, slow it down, or abandon ship if necessary.

Stay spiritual

- Spiritual nourishment comes in many forms. It can be a direct connection with church, prayer, and spiritual readings. Or it can be indirect, like taking a run, lighting a candle in a quiet space, and laughing with friends and family. Tap into your inner wisdom and do whatever it takes for you to find your spiritual center. Stay calm, learn, and observe.

Maintain your responsibilities

• Grappling with change can require a lot of focus. Don't sink your own ship by neglecting your responsibilities. Check on your family and friends. Keep your support system stable. Without that stability, it will be difficult to manage change; the change will manage you.

Find mentors and supporters

• Get to know someone who has managed change successfully. If you learn their skills, you can do the same. For example, if you know someone who grew up in a military family and moved several times, they are probably adept at making new friends. Observe and learn; this is a powerful tool you can use for the rest of your life.

Build resiliency

• You can slow down when you need to, just don't stop. Muscle through your fear when you are worried. Muscle through the pain when your heart is breaking. Muscle through interactions with people when you feel embarrassed, stupid, or insecure. As long as you have agency and resiliency, you can manage change. You may not get everything you want, but you will often find you do have some control over events and how you respond to them.

Teaching Others About Change

Change is an important topic that is missing in our schools. It is critical that students understand that change will happen. Every time I hear of a young adult or teenage suicide, that is what I think of. If they only knew that life will change. Life will change for them because it changes for everybody. The cause of their depression, loneliness or anxiety won't always be there. If they truly understood this, they might find enough faith to hold on until the next change comes.

About the Author

Angela Witcher *is a Certified Public Manager for the New Jersey Department of Environmental Protection, Bureau of GIS. Responsibilities include maintaining a spatial database and applications, providing excellent customer service, and identifying funds for data development. She also has significant experience working on community-based projects, including GIS mentoring and historic preservation. As a volunteer docent, she offers cemetery tours, bringing stories of the past to life for the public.*

your turn...

Use the right tool

When you're faced with change, do you find yourself being the anvil, quietly bearing up? Or do you tend to pick up the hammer?

Think about a time when you had to deal with unwanted change. How did you react? What got you through it? What tools did you use to manage it and push through?

Was there a time you picked up the wrong tool? Were you the hammer when you should have been more resilient? Or maybe you didn't act to change the situation, and wish you had?

Write down your thoughts on the journal pages that follow.

_____

_____

_____

_____

_____

_____

_____

_____

_____

_____

_____

_____

_____

_____

_____

RULE 3
Find Your Allies
by Shea Lemar

When someone tells me a change is coming, I rarely think about the positive outcomes of change, even though there have been so many in my life. Instead, I worry about all the potential unknowns that will be coming and the chaos often associated with new things. I start to worry about different horrible possibilities and imagine all of the unpleasant outcomes (never the positive ones) and I start to get anxious. Even so, I am lucky. I have been through many changes over my life, both good and not so good. And I have learned many valuable lessons about dealing with change, including one that means the most to me. When change is coming or when I am in the midst of it, I gather my groups. I lean on people who will understand my current journey and those I can count on to help me through. I draw comfort and strength from my groups and they help me have hope in the future instead of fearing the unknown.

I don't have just a single person or set of people who support me during times of change. I know people who say they married their best friend and that is the only person they ever need. Kudos to those people. Me? I need more. I am lucky enough to have a wonderful family, an amazing set of friends, and fantastic professional colleagues—and I lean on all of them at different times. But sometimes, I still need more, something else, a new perspective. And when I need them, I find them— sometimes accidentally and sometimes after a lot of work. There is no-one-size-fits-all support person so I find them as I need them, although many times they were there all along ... I just never realized it. As I think back over my life experiences I have found there are a few common types of support groups I depend on when going through major life changes; those with knowledge I can use, those who have shared experiences, and those I know I can count on.

I don't like going into new situations uninformed. I recently started a new role after 24 years at my previous job. I thought I was fairly humble before, but starting a new job can definitely knock your ego down a few notches. I went from being the expert in most everything at my old job to the person who had to ask for help purchasing a monitor. In addition, I was now in charge of major initiatives that I had been aware of, but I needed more in-depth information. I found allies in my new coworkers and in professional colleagues I had worked with over the years. I was able to reach out to them to gain the knowledge I needed to get my job done.

I take the same approach to finding new allies outside the office. When my son was diagnosed with cancer I had no idea what to expect or how to move forward; so I looked to the groups available to help me gain the knowledge I needed. For the medical knowledge, I had the doctors and nurses along with groups created to support people going through these types of situations. We were also able to count on the teachers for the educational support, and other parents who had tips and tricks for understanding our new world. And I have found the ability to learn from others valuable in all sorts of situations. I soon learned, of course, that having knowledge wasn't enough. While we were learning what we needed to do with our son to keep him physically healthy, I didn't realize that my emotional stress levels were shooting up.

We were invited to join a group called HopeKids (www.hopekids.org) the first day my son was diagnosed. I was told that HopeKids provides events, activities, and a support community to families who have a child with cancer and other life-threatening medical conditions. We went to our first event because we thought it would be fun for our boys. I didn't realize until I walked in how powerful it would be to see other people with children wearing masks, in wheel-chairs and using walkers, and any other variety of issues they were dealing with—all while still just being normal families.

For the first time in a long time, I felt normal. Nobody noticed who was bald, nobody cared if someone had tubes coming out of their body, nobody batted an eye if someone got ill. We were surrounded by people who understood what we were going through. They knew what it felt like to be stared at when you walked through the store. They also had to bring their own food when they ate out. And nobody ever noticed or cared or commented on any assortment of bodily issues that would have had us all horribly embarrassed before our lives changed. I had just learned that being around people who had lived through the same experiences I had was life changing. I hear the same thing from people who have gone through divorce, death of a loved one, addiction, and more—being able to speak with others who have your shared experience is incredibly powerful.

As for the people I can count on, they have come from many different places over the years. Some are my family; others are friends I have known since elementary school. Some are college friends, work friends, other GIS people I have gotten to know over years of attending the same conferences, former students, and more. Some are my age, and many are much older or much younger.

Some people I really clicked with and some I didn't. Some are people I see all the time and some are people I rarely see anymore. To be honest, if you had asked me before I met them, I couldn't have predicted which ones would stick and which ones wouldn't. They are all people who accept me, want the best for me, make me laugh, let me cry, and would be there if I called.

As a fairly introverted person, here is the thing that really amazes me. I find the idea of going to conferences or weddings or any large gathering of people pretty daunting and unpleasant. I have friends who are very happily involved in a ton of activities; church, PTA, work, clubs, committees, etc. Whereas my idea of a wonderful weekend is staying in and reading. However, now that I am older I realize over the years I have built up an amazing support team, or teams, without really trying. All of that time spent forcing myself to talk to people at conferences and making a point to grab lunch with a co-worker resulted in a fantastic and unexpected gift. They are just friends and coworkers or sometimes friends of friends ... but when a change comes along and I feel like I need support, I have learned I can turn to different groups of them. Layoffs are coming or the new boss isn't working out? I can reach out to other GIS professionals and my former bosses for job ideas. Moving to a new state? I probably have a friend there, or a friend of a friend, or even my best friend's cousin to help me get to know people. Child diagnosed with cancer? The hospital knows of support groups where I meet parents going through the same thing. As you go through life you connect with people, and you never know which of those people will be the ones you can call on when you are working through a change.

No matter if you are 20 or 80, we all have people we have made some sort of connection with. We share some kind of common bond, some thread that keeps you connected. Those could be the very people you lean on for support when you are experiencing change.

About the Author

Shea Lemar is Arizona's Deputy State Cartographer, specializing in GIS, cartography, and geospatial project management. Formerly GIS Manager at Arizona State University, she provided expert consultation and taught applied GIS. A recognized leader in Arizona's GIS community and active nationally, Shea is passionate about collaboration, education, and advancing geospatial technologies to benefit communities statewide. Her work bridges people, ideas, and innovation, shaping the future of mapping in Arizona.

your turn...

Find your allies

Spend some time now brainstorming where you might find allies for a specific challenge you face. Who might understand what you're going through and be able to help?

Think about people in your life you admire and respect who aren't necessarily close friends. It doesn't matter if it's been many years since you've seen them. Write their names down. These are some of your people ... or they could be. Send them a quick email or text to say hello; maybe plan to grab a coffee or a bite to eat.

Think of conferences and parties as opportunities to connect. Make a point to strike up a conversation when you find potential allies.

If you are currently experiencing a change where you could use some extra support, look for support groups. There are many different groups available for different life events.

Use the journaling space on the following pages to write your thoughts and ideas on who you might connect with.

RULE 4

Mobilize Your Village
by Megan Compton

Change is inevitable—and strong, empathetic leadership during times of change is non-negotiable. Whether it's a career pivot, a shifting team dynamic, changes within the family, a personal challenge, or a societal shift that turns priorities upside down, we all face moments where we must lead, even as we are navigating the changes and finding stable ground ourselves. During the months spent writing this chapter, I have experienced changes in all of these areas in life. It is planned and exciting mixed with unplanned and unnerving. This is a stark reminder that no matter how much challenge and change we have experienced so far, there is more ahead and the effects are unknowable. The realization around every turn reinforces my belief; we are not supposed to do this alone.

Yes, great leaders are calm in the face of change, but that calm isn't manufactured in isolation. It is rooted in hope, perspective, and trust—especially trust in the people you've chosen to be part of your support system, your village. That trust is a two-way street; we earn it by being a leader who shows up, and we cement it by inviting others in. Because you aren't just leading the village. To truly navigate change, you must mobilize your village.

Change, whether personal or professional, rarely gives advance notice. I've experienced this first-hand— from navigating changing traffic patterns that disrupt our commute, to the larger transitions like launching a new career during a period of widespread upheaval. I've seen leadership change overnight and felt what it means when your role, your support, even your job description morphs without warning.

In those moments, it's easy to default to survival mode. But leadership isn't about simply surviving change —it's also about shepherding others through it; minimizing negative impacts; maximizing opportunities. And always pointing to a better outcome, even when the path is uncertain.

When faced with sudden change, before you take a single step ask yourself:

- When this is over, where do I want to be?

- What story do I want others to tell about how we navigated this together?

Having a shared vision for the other side of change gives the people on your team, in your village, something to hold onto. It also reminds you that you're guiding not only processes, but people.

We talk about leaders as visionaries, decision-makers, anchors. But let's not forget the role of *connector*, the liaison who brings together the right people. You don't have to have all the answers. In fact, pretending to will likely erode trust more than build it.

When I've been thrown into challenging situations, whether professionally or personally, my instinct is to handle it—to fix the issue or respond to the need—rather than ask for help. Fortunately at this stage of life, mid-career with a young family, I can attest I have made significant progress in knowing when to call on my village.

Pushing ourselves to figure it out on our own isn't a bad thing; in fact it's a reasonable result of how we were programmed to handle things on our own as we grew into adults.

Maybe you also heard some of these responses as a child asking for help:

"Well, did you look for it before you asked me?"

"Try it on your own and see if you can figure it out."

Knowing how to problem solve and navigate solo is so important. Yet humans also need to know that asking for help is not defeat. The times I've felt the most grounded were the times I actively reached out to those around me. From quick gut checks with colleagues, to leaning on my family and friends when making a tough decision—these weren't signs of weakness. They were signs of wisdom.

Your people—your team, family, community, trusted peers—want to help. But they often won't unless you ask. That's not a lack of loyalty; it's human nature. Most people don't want to step on toes or get in the way. So make it clear—their insight is not just welcome, it's essential. This is true in my relationship with the most influential mentor in my life thus far. Even after knowing each other and collaborating for more than 15 years, there are still times when they can see I need help before I ask, and often before I even recognize that I need it. Having an open door policy, along with humility and an openness to be challenged with new thoughts, will encourage input from others around you. That input from your village is invaluable!

Leaders—whether leading a family, a work team, or a community project—don't walk ahead; they walk with, side by side, ideally with a shared vision of a good outcome. Mobilizing your village and being an active connector doesn't make you less of a leader; it makes you a more *effective* one.

Do the next right thing

There's a moment in the Disney movie *Frozen 2* when Anna, lost in grief and uncertainty, sings "just do the next right thing." It's simple. Profound. And a perfect strategy for navigating change. (Anderson-Lopez and Lopez, 2019).

When a situation shifts dramatically—when a path closes, or your goalposts move without notice—your plans may fall apart. You may not know what to do three steps from now. But you *can* identify one right move. That next call, that one conversation, that small but positive step forward.

I've learned this lesson in both subtle and visceral ways. Taking the next step, and then another, to finish a race while injured and ill. I couldn't think about the finish line—I just had to make it to the next marker. Or an impromptu adventure climbing Michigan's Sleeping Bear Dunes at dusk, with a storm looming and the only way out being up. There was no time for a five-step plan. Just one step, then another.

In leadership, whether that be in your community or at work, the clarity to focus on the next right thing can be your lifeline—and your team's anchor. Let them see your humanity. Let them see your process. And always keep your eyes on what's possible, not just what's painful and immediate.

Establish your new baseline

Even while we focus on the next right thing, when change comes at us fast everything can feel distorted. The ground beneath your feet may no longer be solid. That's why it's critical to establish your new baseline.

Where are you *really*? What are the known facts? What's noise and what's signal?

Even if you had a perfect handle on the situation before, check in again. All along your journey, you should constantly be aware of your location in reference to everything around you; knowing where you started, where you are, and where you are headed. If you get knocked off the rocks on your climb, your new starting point is where you have landed. Now you have set that new baseline, take stock of what is around you, recognize what you know about your environment. Do you still know where you are headed? Has the new environment changed your destination? Do your instruments still work?

It's also important to remember that not all change is catastrophic. Your reaction doesn't need to be scaled to your discomfort. Know the difference.

Gather the data, then decide

Even as we come to terms with our new baseline, acting without full information is sometimes necessary. But rushing to action with incomplete data is generally a recipe for regret. If the situation is unclear, don't panic—pause.

Close the data gap. Ask questions. Consult your village. Look at the full scope. Not every change calls for urgency. Sometimes, the most powerful decision is to wait until the picture sharpens.

Research and analysis of the NASA space shuttle Challenger disaster and the decisions that led up to the launch—decisions made with missing, misread, or ignored data—reveal the critical need to obtain as much information as possible and continue to seek answers. (Qian, 2020). It's a haunting reminder: When lives or livelihoods are on the line, take the time to get the facts.

Seek clarity

Sometimes, clarity is just a higher vantage point away. You may need to climb—mentally, physically, or emotionally—to see the full picture. Change doesn't just impact the goal; it often rewrites the rules. When this happens, an effective leader must be willing to pivot, and help your village make that pivot with you.

The key is not to abandon all ideas, but to hold them loosely. Some strategies may not serve you *now*, but could become essential *later*. Don't discard them—shelve them for the time being. Every leader has a toolbox full of ideas. Keep yours fully stocked, and open it fully when the need arises.

During the COVID-19 pandemic, the team I was leading (and our broader geospatial community) were concerned about the future of a well-respected and highly-utilized but poorly-resourced spatial data library. Quick fixes to maintain the status quo were the most reasonable approach, given the current circumstances and their impact on all levels of decision making. Yet despite many unknowns, I envisioned an approach that wouldn't require us to settle for quick fixes. I believed we could elevate the spatial data library utilization, especially critical in that time when location information and data was in such high demand.

In late 2020, I invited some close colleagues to an outdoor white-board session in my backyard—a reasonable solution given the risks of spreading the virus. We were no strangers to big ideas and enjoyed throwing the proverbial spaghetti to see what would stick. After several hours we had drawn out a new spatial data library solution and workflow. We were not sure how each piece would fit together, yet by pulling from our shared experience and dropping the notion of "this is how we have always done it," the outcome was ultimately wildly successful.

While change on its surface can look messy, it often serves to clear the clutter, making space for opportunities. Be alert to those openings. They can often be the catalyst for real progress on a long-held goal.

Just remember – big decisions shouldn't happen in a vacuum. When possible, pre-wire the plan. Share your thinking early, build consensus, and listen—*really* listen—to the voices around you. This does two things:

1. It sharpens your decision-making with real-world input; and

2. It turns stakeholders into partners.

I experienced the impact of failing to put the right people around the decision table early on in my career, near the time I shifted some focus from public safety and deeper into geography and technology. I was selected for a new position in 2014 to update and deploy new critical datasets and navigation tools for a large public safety agency. The system had been built and deployed before I arrived, which meant my approach needed to fit within the limitations of the existing solution. The process was fragmented, misunderstood by the end-users, and the solution timeline was many months longer than necessary. That lesson engrained the criticality of bringing in the right people early on in a project, so the tough options can be discussed and consensus built before it is too late.

People are far more likely to support what they've helped shape. Even if they don't agree 100% with the plan, being invited into the process builds trust and shared ownership. For example, I had the opportunity to redesign a large information technology infrastructure and rebuild the platform. This happened at a time when systems had become more web-capable, hybrid technology solutions were more feasible, and everyone wanted to move into the cloud. Several teams and resources depended on our solution being reliable and efficient, nearly unbreakable. We deliberately engaged the people and teams that were most directly impacted, those who would be the most critical of our design, and colleagues with unique expertise and strong reputations. The solution ultimately designed and adopted was created by people who were not the usual suspects. Their diversity of thought and vision supported a titanic-level shift and created lasting partnerships that had a positive impact on future projects.

When people feel seen and heard, they rise. Every time.

True leadership means considering your impact on others, in all you do. This is deeply personal for me. I strive to understand how my decisions will ripple out. Especially now, in a world that sometimes feels too fast, too loud, and too self-centered, I believe leaders must be radically considerate. We must be cognizant and considerate of the change that others are experiencing too.

Change doesn't just affect you. It touches your team, your colleagues, your family. It may trigger something in them — fear, loss, hope, excitement. Don't assume everyone feels what you feel. Be intentional about getting their pulse, checking in on how they're doing.

So slow down. Look around. Consider the second- and third-order impacts of your choices. What may seem small or logical to you could be a seismic shift for someone else.

True leaders, especially in times of significant change, respect the power of empathy.

There's a beautiful moment in the book "Into the Wild" where the protagonist learns—too late—that "happiness is only real when shared." Humans truly are not meant to go it alone. (Krakauer, 1996.)

When you commit to mobilizing your village, you become part of someone else's village, too. This creates a powerful feedback loop of support and trust, and the beauty of that loop is that it does not end. The people and groups you support and mobilize will come back around someday to help mobilize you. What if that happens when you least expect it? If you lean into that support and trust the loop, you may be surprised when it comes back around and you grab onto that lifeline, instead of pulling it for others.

I've been carried by others through major life changes, and I've carried others in my turn. That's the rhythm of leadership and of love created by mindfully enlisting your village; receiving and giving, holding and being held.

If you follow this approach, please be willing to lift people on their terms, not on yours.

This rhythm played out in my life and relationships over the course of a few years, with two major life events in particular. In 2016, my husband and I delivered a baby girl at 32 weeks, and she did not survive. That experience is indescribably overwhelming and it is nearly impossible to know what you need or what to do. The support we received was extraordinary, more than I can put into this chapter. One key effort came from dear friends who helped organize food for our family and support for our eldest daughter, who was almost two years old. They supported us with what we needed, while respecting our space for grieving.

A few years later, these same friends experienced a terrible accident that nearly destroyed their beautiful and historic family home. Our actions to support the family, including their teenage daughter, came without hesitation. We mobilized quickly and supported them with what they needed, which changed week-to-week. As a support structure we had to adapt and listen, understand when they needed things and consider how they needed to receive it, being mindful to make it on their terms.

No one leads for one. Not really. When you lean in with authenticity, others will join. Not because they have to. Because they want to. Learn to be willing to be supported by others, accepting that you can't do it on your own.

Sometimes though, you don't know the answer. Sometimes, the terrain keeps shifting and you're building the plane mid-flight. That's okay—if you handle those moments with confidence and humility.

Take the pulse of what *is* true. Anchor yourself in values, facts, and intentions. You don't need every variable solved. You just need to move forward in truth.

And in those moments, lean on your people. They will remind you of your strength ... and theirs.

Get comfortable with being uncomfortable

One final thought: Leading through change will put you in rooms you don't feel ready for. You may be the youngest. The only woman. The only person from your background, your discipline, your lens.

I've been the public safety expert chosen to lead skilled technologists and professional geographers. The civilian delivering the keynote address for a conference of sworn law enforcement and military. The woman leading a team of all men. The slowest rider in a cycling club. The outsider in a room of insiders. Imposter syndrome doesn't knock—it barges right in and takes the best chair. But I've learned something: Discomfort is not a signal to retreat. It's often a sign **you're right where you're supposed to be**. Get comfortable with being uncomfortable and bring your village with you.

Don't let the discomfort of change—of true leadership —shrink you. Let it stretch you. Then, help stretch others too. Face your discomfort and ask for help when you need it. Your village will rally to your side in ways you can't imagine. And they will be honored to help and grateful you asked.

Because what change has ultimately taught me is this: We are truly not meant to face it alone.

About the Author

Megan Compton is a public sector leader with 18 years of experience guiding teams across geospatial, technology, public safety, and research sectors. As the Senior Advisor for the Federal Geographic Data Committee, she helps guide national geospatial strategy and deepen cross-sector engagement that is rooted in her recent tenure as a State Geographic Information Officer. Like a skilled navigator, she excels at finding the right path, assembling the right team, and reaching higher than expected. A sought-after speaker and award-winning collaborator, Megan has a gift for connecting people and ideas to achieve strategic and impactful goals. She is passionate about advancing women in leadership and technology and leads initiatives with Government Women in Technology and GeoWomen. An Indiana University alumna, she lives near Indianapolis and can often be found with her family in outdoor activities or traveling.

your turn...

Mobilize your village

Think of a change you are facing now. Before you take the next, step ask yourself: *When this is over, where do I want to be? What story do I want others to tell about how I navigated this?*

Who do you need to bring in to make that story come true? Can you ask for help from your family? Friends? Colleagues? How does the idea of asking for help make you feel?

Now think about how this change might impact the people in your village. How can you bring them in while being empathetic to their needs?

Can you work toward that beautiful rhythm of giving and receiving help, with leadership and love?

Use the following journal pages to write down your thoughts.

_____

_____

_____

_____

_____

_____

_____

_____

_____

_____

_____

_____

_____

_____

_____

_____

_____

_____

_____

_____

_____

_____

_____

_____

_____

_____

_____

_____

_____

RULE 5
Prioritize, then Adapt
by Erin Fashoway

Life has an interesting way of resetting your priorities. We have all been through change in our lives, whether sudden or planned, welcome or unwelcome. The birth of a child, a wedding, a death after a long cancer fight, job loss due to major budget cuts—regardless of the type of change, positive or negative, it's a disruption to work and life flow. And we all know the saying "change is hard." It's a cliche because it's true. Sudden change can take all our well-intentioned priorities and throw them out the window.

The little rule I have found most helpful when dealing with change is to be able to adapt and redefine my priorities in real time. When life throws those inevitable changes your way, be ready to adapt and reprioritize. My mantra? Prioritize, adapt, reprioritize, wash, rinse, repeat.

As a younger woman, I used written lists to set my priorities. I developed this habit to help me get organized and define what was most important to me. List making was my young-adult way to handle change; it was a habit that made sense to the way my younger brain worked. As a 40-something, mother of two, wife, and full-time professional, I have learned that being able to adapt and reset priorities is a good strategy for reducing risk while trying to deal with the impact of change.

Define Your Priorities

There are many different ways to define your priorities in life. First, I recommend doing a brain dump on paper by writing them all down. Simply by completing this task you will begin to eliminate some priorities or spark new ideas. Having trouble defining your priorities or need some advice on what you are trying to achieve? Bring in your trusted tribe, the people who give you sound guidance or offer a nonjudgmental ear; your spouse, parents, colleagues, mentors, other family, or friends. These are the people in your life you can be vulnerable with or have life experiences you want to learn from.

Brain dump complete, it's time to get organized! I find most of my priorities are important and urgent. What should be completed or started urgently or what is the most important? What is not important or what is not urgent? The items that fall under important and urgent can be prioritized at the top of your list. Next could be the urgent and not important items. And so on and so forth, other items fall into place along the way.

A simple way to look at this is the Eisenhower Matrix; four quadrants, where you can sort what needs to be done by importance and urgency. (Gupta, 2025)

EISENHOWER MATRIX

	Urgent	Not Urgent
Important	DO	DECIDE
Not Important	DELEGATE	DELETE

Of course there are always times when we have to bump one priority for another. Recently, I was traveling for work where a colleague and I were conducting outreach interviews of our stakeholders. We had about two months to conduct roughly 15 in-person interviews across the state of Montana (172,000 sq. miles) and analyze the results of our work ... all while juggling summer schedules with our kids. The results were to be presented to our executive team and governing body. I had classified this as both an urgent and an important work priority.

On Day Two of a three day trip, I started getting text messages from my husband; our son (who has a chronic condition) was not well. While this trip was the first round of three cross-state trips we had planned on conducting (I knew this was urgent/important), I prioritized my son's wellbeing above my work priorities. My colleague and I had to quickly pivot. We were able to cancel reservations, immediately drive home, and cancel an interview, with the intention of rescheduling within the two-month timeframe we had been given. My urgent and most important priority for the remainder of that week was my family. We had priorities set, life came at us, we adapted and moved forward.

Another example, this time in my professional life, took place in 2017. The department I work for experienced significant budget cuts. Within our work team we lost four of our team members along with other key supportive staff; across the entire department we lost over 20% of our staff. We had annual work plans in place, but nothing prepared us for such a giant loss of staff; we were forced to go back to the basics and adapt. We had to re-prioritize and re-examine most of everything we did. We worked with our teams to understand what was urgent and what was important. We had to let go of a lot of the old norms and work cultures we had gotten used to. The silver lining to this process was unexpected; we had to get much better at quickly saying no and defining what our team needed to accomplish, all while staying on top of the budget. After immediately going into survival mode, we went through a strategic planning process to define our three and five year goals and our major priorities. We worked with the partners we served to define their needs, examined our own policies and procedures, and developed a path forward—all while surviving some pretty rough change.

Embrace the clarity of the moment

Have you ever had a moment of clarity during an emergency situation, where all noise and distractions disappear? You knew exactly what to do and what order to do it in, because what truly mattered quickly rose to the surface. In that moment, everything became abundantly crystal clear. We need to learn to lean into those moments of clarity.

One very memorable moment of clarity came to me during the COVID-19 pandemic. The pandemic really changed the way I understood basic human needs and maxed me to my limits in so many different ways. The first few months of the pandemic were extremely stressful for me. I was working long and intense hours, working over weekends, answering to high elected officials and the press. I was part of a small team that was responsible for creating and updating infection/

death rates of the virus. Every day I watched cases rise and fall, new death tolls be tallied and applied to our maps and dashboards. I cried at my desk when I saw the first infant death being reported. All of this took a major emotional toll, yet I prided myself on doing the best I could to provide the public with resources they could rely upon. I took it very seriously and felt it was an incredible honor and responsibility.

During those first few weeks, I prioritized my fellow citizens. It was a disaster response. Our support staff reset their priorities too, reminding us to eat, take breaks, get fresh air, ask for help ... they were amazing. I leaned into my work harder than I ever have in my life. We had built a camaraderie with our small group, together responding and making a difference.

Eventually, the emergency operations center decentralized and we were ordered to work remotely from homes. I continued to work hard from home, responding to the disaster. Being at home brought new priorities, as the line between work and home became nearly transparent. Trying to give snuggles to my son and my dog. Trying to give attention to my husband/best friend. Trying to take good care of myself in all of it. In many ways, being work-obsessed was a great distraction from the madness that the world had fallen into around me, but I missed my team. I was one of the lucky ones who was able to continue to work from an office at the beginning, but I really felt the isolation with the shift to home.

Another thing you should know about me is that I am an extreme extrovert, practically off the charts. I process the world through speaking and being with people. After being locked down for several weeks, I started to realize I didn't just need to speak with people; I needed to be physically around people. Essentially, I needed a hug. I will never forget the day, about four weeks into the pandemic, when I stopped off at my best friend's house who lives about five minutes away from me to say hi. We had agreed in advance to be the defined distance apart. Yet as soon as I saw her, I felt the urge to give her a giant best friend bear hug! She knew it and, of course, obliged.

In that instant I felt overwhelming relief and comfort. It was clear what I needed. At the time it might not have been recommended, but my family and hers decided to create our own little COVID pod; we were loyal to keeping our distances from others to keep us all safe. We chose to prioritize being with each other's families—to see and interact with each other in-person—in spite of the risks. My best friend and I have adopted each other's families as our own, with a shared history that goes back years and no family for either of us nearby.

I consider myself a curious person and because of identifying personal contact as a major priority in my life, I have done research on the power of a hug. As silly as this may seem, my daily priority is to be sure I give my sons at least two big hugs, lasting eight seconds to be exact. Why eight seconds you may ask? Well I probably read that eight seconds leaves some lasting impact, but I like to think of hugging them sometimes like hugging a wild bronc and you just got to hang on! From what I hear, as they grow older they will need me just a little less ... so in the meantime I will prioritize my sons' hugs with a yeehaw!! As for the data, scientists have found a link between hugs and lower stress hormones the next day. (Romney, 2023).

So if priorities are liable to shift at a moment's notice, why do we define them at all? What I've realized is this: no matter what you do you are always inadvertently prioritizing some life activity, work task, or someone above another. This creates a habit of constantly putting something (some activity, someone, some work task, some life task) above something else. Without a good strategy in place or a good examination of what needs to be accomplished at a certain point in time, you might be just avoiding your priorities instead of tackling them. It is much easier to plan or strategize in advance well before things are in the midst of a major change.

Use Your Tools

Now that you've written down your priorities and categorized them, don't lose sight of all your hard work!

It's time to document and visualize your priorities, using whatever tool resonates with you! Having your priorities in front of you or quickly accessible will make it less likely to forget or avoid them. Even better, you have the satisfaction of checking something off or seeing progress being made! I've used lots of different tools and I found these approaches helpful:

1. *Good old-fashioned pen and paper.*
Never underestimate the powerful impact of writing something down. Personally, I'm able to better commit things to memory this way; studies have shown that writing something down significantly increases retention of knowledge over typing (Hu, 2024). Get yourself a pretty notebook— leather bound or sparkles or whatever suits you— and keep it handy for writing down your thoughts and ideas while you're going through change.

2. *Embrace spreadsheets.*
No matter what you need to prioritize, you'll find so many different templates already pre-made for priorities, budgets plans, project plans, you name it; they're just all there at your disposal if you only look. Whether you use a Microsoft spreadsheet, a Google sheet or Apple Numbers, spreadsheets are powerful. You can sort things by timelines, you can sort items by costs or whatever other metric is important. A good spreadsheet allows the user to visualize what needs to be accomplished or what

information they're trying to relay; and it's a bonus that you can share these digitally with friends and partners, coworkers, etc. and pass the information back and forth. I also highly recommend using colors to sort through or demarcate things that are overdue, or perhaps things that are really important, or items that are going to cost more money than you originally budgeted. With a good spreadsheet the world is your oyster and I believe anybody can create a beautiful spreadsheet.

3. *There's an app for that!*
I have used many different types of apps to organize my priorities in my daily tasks, to set reminders and to help keep me organized both in my work and personal lives. I've explored taskmasters for children to help my kiddos with organization and reminders too. They can be free or behind a paywall. My recommendation is to read reviews, do some research, be open minded, and try something new!

Celebrate your successes

When reviewing and resetting your priorities, don't forget to self-reflect. Mourn and embrace the times you failed; learn from your past experiences and celebrate the successes! Do this with family, friends, or work colleagues. As humans, we have so much to learn from our failures and our challenges. We learn how to adapt, how to pivot, how to research a topic to learn what we need to move forward. It would be a lovely life if everything came easy, but I believe it's in challenges that we build our true muscle, proving to ourselves that we can adapt to whatever comes our way. And it's just as important to give ourselves that high five when we've finished that tough assignment, submitted that draft, made that pivot and reworked priorities and leaned into whatever's next.

One final thought ... for the mothers, the overworked managers, the older sisters and brothers, the working parents, the sandwich generation taking care of two generations at once ... indeed all you amazing caretakers. You know who you are. I hope you prioritize yourself through this process. Take the time to prioritize your needs and desires. Your health and your well being should be listed as very important; you are the hub it all revolves around. Remember, you are no good to others, the ones you take care of, if you are not well.

About the Author

Erin Fashoway *has worked in the geospatial industry for over 20 years. She calls the Rocky Mountain west her home. She is a mother, sister, friend, & wife. When her kiddos or job aren't keeping her busy, Erin loves to spend time with friends and family outside enjoying mountain culture.*

your turn...

Prioritize, then adapt

Do you find yourself prioritizing things based on other people's needs? If you're a parent, the answer is no doubt yes ... but what about co-workers who need something now for their work? Or that friend who can't wait another minute for you to help with her problem? What tactics can you use to stop making someone else's urgency your problem?

What tools do you find most helpful in getting organized and reprioritized? Paper and pen? To-do apps? Other? How can you use your current methods across more areas of your life?

Think about the interruptions and time wasters in your life; are there things you find yourself spending time on that someone else could or should handle? What about the things that are neither urgent nor important, like sorting through junk mail? How can you streamline or eliminate those things from your routine?

Jot down your thoughts on the following pages.

_____

_____

_____

_____

_____

_____

_____

_____

_____

_____

_____

_____

_____

RULE 6

Embrace the Imperfect
by Natalie Lee

These days, it really can feel like the goal posts are moving on you. Particularly in balancing family and career—everyone wants (and needs) a piece of you, and the moment you think you've figured out a new system, or let your "hustle" down for a moment, there is more to do, to pursue, to fine tune. I work from home, which in theory means I have more margin between the two and thus can seamlessly move from work to home life. Dreamy!

In reality, they both are constantly vying for my brain and passion. Any moment I COULD be doing laundry or catching up on emails or writing something or organizing something for the kids' school or laundry or

... the list goes on. There is always the possibility of catching up on one or the other, yet no one is ever (ever) satisfied.

I remember once having a cranky kiddo literally hanging onto my chair desperate for my attention while a colleague (also desperate) needed me via teleconference around dinner time one evening. My husband came in the door and, not realizing I was on a call, oblivious to the adorable need machine climbing onto my lap to assert himself, started to chat me up about the news of the day. An overstimulated me lost it. I remember telling my colleague tersely that I needed to take a break and then SHOUTING at my husband something unintelligible about the situation and my need for HELP and also something like "Is this the dream?! WHY do I bother trying?!! I NEED A TIMEOUT!" I probably spent the evening in our room with a glass of wine and some chocolate I had squirreled away in my bedside table. I also probably snuck in an email or two before bed.

For those us who have grown up learning to put their best foot forward, to show up prepared, to break those glass ceilings ... to prove that putting you on the team was worth it, that you aren't going to give your kids THAT much for their therapist, the constant pursuit of perfection at home and at work is exhausting, impossible, and alienating. In my experience, embracing imperfection and inviting others into this madness, while enjoying the chaos of it all, is really the only way.

The truth is, society (and that includes us) really is moving the goal post on us, and it's totally normal to spend an inordinate amount of time saying the words "This is all too much right now." A gallop poll recently reported that 50% of women feel "stressed." (Barry et. al., 2024). That tracks, right?

According to Pew Research Center (Fry, 2023), 71% of the household duties are still performed by women, despite a positive trend of 88% of adults believing that parenting responsibilities should be shared equally. Precious!

Women are also choosing the workforce in increasing numbers; the US Department of Labor estimated in 2024 that 88% of U.S. mothers with children under 18 were either employed or actively seeking work, up from 58.9% in 1983. We've all heard these sorts of numbers before, but what it means for us, the women in the trenches managing both family and career, is the expectations might be changing, but the workload persists in both spaces. It's a lot.

The good news for those of us experiencing the constant upheaval of parenting while working is that we have insider knowledge that can (and should) be shared. We all have a particular set of skills that, when tapped into, can help us lead others and ourselves through the murky seasons of career and home. We have a whole lot to offer. And while the chaos of our lives in this season makes us FEEL like "too much," embracing the chaos offers an important perspective and makes us accessible and real.

Let me start by validating, from personal experience, that in the Year of our Lord 2025, being a working mother for many is physically, emotionally and mentally untenable. The comedian Jim Gaffigan talks about how the feeling of having five children is like drowning and then having someone hand you a baby. When I heard that the first time, probably somewhere between my first and second kid, I thought to myself "that's working motherhood..."

The truth, which many have explored from both sides, is somewhere between two extremes: "You can have it all!" and "Find a way to be happy in one or the other but stop trying to win at both." As we swing between these two ideologies like a sweaty exhausted acrobat from a knockoff Cirque du Soleil performance, we strive for the elusive happy medium. The swinging happens as we react to finding ourselves in periods of change because the only thing more sure than whether a successful hit band will reunite for "one more tour" is this—kids change. And with those changes come changes for us too. Just as we find a groove or report out at a girls' weekend that "I think we have figured out something that works for us!" give it a minute ... because a change inevitably follows, rendering us back at the proverbial drawing board.

By the time you have an elementary schooler, you become accustomed to this "what shoe will drop next?" routine. Each time we hit a patch of smooth water, we evaluate: "Is this a time where we are going to find that sweet spot of life/work contentment?" Those thoughts happen just about the time the school nurse calls to inform us that our kid has thrown up and "could we come back and grab them please and thank you?" Back to chaos, we think. Home sweet home.

The solution, we are told, is that we need more margins, more of a village, more intentionality, more peace in the chaos! I would offer that all of that is true ... and also ... to navigate the choppy waters of parenthood and career in my own experience is to embrace the messy imperfection and see where you can invite others in by being brutally honest about it.

There are more times than I can count when I have failed by conventional standards in this journey, and I'm not even sort of close to being done. At the time I am writing, I have three children: 14, 10, and 6. All three of my kids are dynamic and funny and smart. They are spicy in all the ways that people tell you will "set them up for greatness" and also ... So. Many. Needs. They deserve a mother who is present and intentional about their lives and trajectories and I am so here for all of that for all three of them. And also ... I'm tired and "Can Mommy please have a minute to sit, untouched, without watching that thing you just unlocked on your computer game or reliving through your dynamic retelling the meme of that person you told me about last week when we were on the way to the pool?" It is unrelenting.

Friends of mine once gave a lecture, complete with charts that demonstrated the years of parenting with a huge section colored in brown with the words "Poop Years," a reminder I chuckle at every time things get a little bit too hard. The Poop Years span the literal years of diaper changing and reach into these years of the "sludge" and grind of shuffling and reminding and cleaning and disinfecting and reorganizing as our children change and grow by leaps and bounds. As they change, I find myself and my husband changing too; pivoting as we greet each dynamic change brought to us by these three need machines and their ... New! Creative! Novel! ways of upending what might have seemed to be working (for the last couple weeks at least).

We just want to keep them alive ... and we also want them to be fully-fledged independent world changers too. No one in prison would be great. Also maybe someone in the White House? Children help us change our ideologies, as we are exposed to new ways of thinking, and we are challenged and questioned in all the ways that (hopefully) make us new and wise and useful. The modifications of our own ideas and system—how we work, how we produce, how we connect, how we affirm—are as useful to our work as to our parenting. There is so much good overlap. The change is so important, even as it is exhausting and can make us feel rudderless. The Poop Years promise one thing: When we come out on the other side (bad choice of words) we will be different, and we will have experienced as many iterations of ourselves as our kids.

For those of us in the Poop Years of our careers, a similar experience perhaps occurs. These are the building years. We have charted the general career course, and know, we think, where we ultimately want to go. We are putting in the time to learn and be mentored and get those experiences to help us to make it to that dream job where we can make that dream impact. While change is not necessarily a hallmark of this period (but maybe it is?), it seems cosmically hilarious that right about the time we are at this point of transitioning from mentee to mentor, worker bee to architect and director, some of us have also entered a similar set of new challenges in the Poop Years at home. At this point, a decade or two into your career, you are offered leadership about the time you start having kids. Every expectation you had about parenting is upended, your worldview is tested, your concept of how you were raised redefined, and your experience of the world modified. Here you sit, "ready" to be the person who can speak wisdom to a situation, to lead a group confidently into a new data program or project ... and you find yourself thinking "I can't even get my toddler to stop streaking across the lawn."

There is so much to say about the overlaps between mothering and leadership (e.g, talking to a wayward contractor is not unlike gentle parenting one's toddler). If change is inevitable and leadership is in store for you (and honestly, it is for every parent), it's good news that we can let some of these tips and tricks do double duty.

Perhaps the most useful saying to me at this juncture is to acknowledge that perfection is the enemy of good; not only because perfection is unattainable, but because sometimes (not always) the very pursuit of it is a way to find yourself in a one-woman show.

I am very lucky to be part of a group of women in my field. We fiercely advocate for each other. We cheerlead, we brainstorm, and we invite others in, period. Are you new to us? Wonderful, we are glad you came. We consider the wisdom of the women who came before us, in our circles and in the broader world of smart women. We only see each other a few times a year, but keep up over text and by phone in between. While not all of us are mothers, many of us are, and there is support there too. We laugh at the common experiences and foibles.

When I joined that space, I was so struck by the unspoken rule—there is no room for ego or sidelining.

None of us demonstrated (or tried to portray) perfection. Rather, there was a (usually lighthearted and self-deprecating) invitation into the challenge or win of the moment. What a lesson and refreshing time it is, to be with others who invite others in with sincerity and camaraderie.

Especially for those in the building years, inviting others into the work is so important and rewarding. I know I am not alone in this either. When it comes to finding and joining people in their work, two things keep me coming back; humility and creativity! I find it exciting being invited into something because it's not done yet. In truth, that level of honesty, the ability to stay true and honest even when no one is watching, and invite others into the chaos, is amazing.

This is not falsely feigning or humble bragging ("Oh I am such a mess ... I only baked cookies for everyone and wrote a 42 page prep document for this meeting!"). We all know those people. It is not safe to put your guard down around them because you know they are just going to feast on your mess the moment they turn the corner. They can't let you help because the bar they set for themselves is so high, they can't risk you helping. I've found myself in that routine before too—the moment I think I've got it together and I have found the solution and I'm really the only person who can do it, we are sunk. No, real humility is a pursuit and position of curious research, making note of where you might be falling short and where you think things could be improved. Humility's sister is creativity, because in the examination of what might be "not optimal" is the wide door to the possible. Messy can be so much fun, and can lead to such interesting things!

With our guards down and our embrace of where we really are, we can pivot and think outside the box in a new and exciting way. Without the humble acknowledgement of what is not, you cannot imagine what could be.

Like my co-authors, I'm a geographer. The study of people and place and their relationships to each other has fascinated me since childhood. My work is exciting and rewarding as I build data and maps with people in lots of different disciplines with the goal of making the world, and specifically my state, a better place to live and work and grow in. Creativity and collaboration are the hallmarks of a good geographer. We are equal parts innovators and doers, and the best of us are connected and collaborating all the time with people across the nation and world. We are constantly dreaming up new ways to work with people and get things done. And as climate and culture and political power change, we change too, pivoting to do our work and continue to make the world a better place.

For me, this prioritization of collaboration and innovation began with my father. I am the daughter of a photographic scientist and sometimes geographer who was, to me, a real life MacGyver. Dad was always creating a new jig or platform or attachment, whether at home or at work, to make something work or get something from A to B. A scientist for the Navy, he was constantly thinking and sketching. When he retired, a young person who was in his old job called him up and asked "Hey Chris, where did you get that thing?" My Dad said humbly, "Oh, I made that."

The way he tells the story there was some silence on the other line as the young thing tried to sort out what that meant, then "Oh! How?" Dad would tell them about some scrap metal and wood in a closet where he stored away bits and pieces, and how he would put things together to make something new that would help get the job done. Never gatekeeping knowledge from anyone and always happy to share what kept the thing from being ideal, he invited the next person to do even better. His work, like mine, was the constant exciting world of problem solving with a team; always a new thing to build or explore, always a new person to understand and work with (or around!).

It has become a habit to approach parenting and career in that same way; through the relentless changes of situation and growth, I'm always searching for a way to think outside the box, and stay honest about what's not working right now. There are so many more people in my village when I am honest about what's going off the rails right now and what I'm trying to figure out. I like to think we are pioneering new ways of doing the work of building data and programs and raising contributing members of society—in the same way that people dreamt up Teen Uber and Instacart. In a very real way the simple act of being vulnerable enough to acknowledge the mess before you changes the chemistry of our minds and shifts us into a new space ... and perhaps in the midst of change that's really the best way to move into smoother seas.

I think I can pinpoint the moment I embarked on this journey of "embracing the mess." At 24 weeks, things went off the rails with my first pregnancy. Up until this point I was able (in my own imperfect estimation) to do all the things and do them to the nth degree. At this point the demands of work were really not inconveniencing my career, and my OCD (legit and not yet well managed) was making it possible for me to hyper focus and catch and deal with things out of place in my work. I was even applying this same level of "extra" to my personal weight-loss goals. Add personal privilege and a college degree with a job that allowed me to pay it off slowly but surely and I was doing OK. While not a Rothschild, I was able to present a relatively polished demeanor and do the things.

Parenthood, I was convinced, would of course be hard and challenging or whatever ... but my husband and I were smart and driven and doing all the "right things" as prescribed by my church, doctor, and cultural tradition. Imagine my surprise as I was wheeled into the high risk prenatal wing of Northside Hospital in Atlanta. How long? No idea. Could we prevent her from being born too early? We don't know. Will she be OK? We hope so, but she needs more time. We had about four and a half weeks in all to come to reckon with both the miracle of life and my utter inability to bend the new stage to what I expected and thought was manageable.

At 29 weeks, she was born. She was, like her mother I like to think, a feisty little thing. She was instantly unique and beautiful; we were so in love with her. She (and we) did all of the ups and downs of preemie-hood. Two steps forward, one step back was a NICU phrase my husband and I learned. "Stay positive, embrace the journey, it's a marathon" were all things said to us by angelic nurses and friends who had been through it before. Meanwhile, one—maybe even the biggest—pivot and unknown of my life unfolded. I grieved hard and raw and openly; not only was I grieving the pregnancy and birth experience I had expected, but the life I thought we would have was now completely different. I was a mother to a (for now) medically fragile kiddo, a working mother with things to keep afloat somehow while I managed all of the worry and anxiety of that new role while managing my career and responsibilities at work. I struggled to connect with this new chapter and my daughter, both terrified that she would be taken from me (what could I depend on? Nothing was going like I thought!) and desperate to get to "do motherhood" the way I thought in my head it should be done.

Naturally, I turned to books and blogs and people who seemed to have things figured out. My favorites were women who talked candidly about the missteps and chaos of this life stage. I was drawn to women who were self deprecating and honest. I noticed a theme though: The shiny polished look was still selling ... there weren't a lot of working women talking about how to make these years work. There seemed to be a lot of white knuckling and amnesia, people putting their careers on hold while they had their children. It was all very rewarding and they got through it somehow but then they went back to work and that's where the story picks up. Or they didn't and that's where the story picked up.

For a lot of us, that's not an option. Not only because physically and financially it's impossible, but because leaving our profession for a time means becoming out of touch with it altogether; by the time you come back things will have changed so much that you've been rendered unmarketable. (There's something to say about what happens when women choose to help propagate the human race and how they are punished for daring to return to work after, but that's a topic for another day.)

So my husband and I graduated from the NICU with our wonderful daughter. She brought to our lives all the fear and fun and joy we were promised. We changed how we prioritized work, certainly; imperfectly ebbing and flowing with what she needed and what our careers needed to keep moving forward. I can remember excitedly telling my best friends about new hacks for making the things work together. Even still, we would sometimes admit to each other that things were rough, our hacks not always hacking it, and that we needed to think through a new option or tweak to our realities ... or we needed a serious jump in cloning technology.

Those were the moments we weathered together in harmony, thinking through each other's issues and considering new avenues for how things could be. In some ways, the utter leveling of my parenting expectations in the first six months of my daughter's life prepped me to receive the pivots that would come, to be more comfortable in imperfection. Nothing was going to go as planned. No one was going to have an easy answer. Anyone who said they had it together was hiding something or about to crash. The future was unknown.

So, I started to learn (kicking and screaming the whole way) to hold things with an open hand, and invite the chaos of life—it was coming anyway. I accepted that I wouldn't be able to hold together a lifestyle or "way" that other people were going to want to follow. I was already unable to keep up a façade.

To be fair, I think in a lot of ways I wanted that. I wanted to be extraordinary—maybe everyone does—and

I wanted to live a life that projected I had things together. My husband would say that I still do, requiring what he would say is unattainable cleanliness before a dinner party or lamenting the school photos where my daughter went through her "White Snake Hair Era." And he's probably right; I am still holding tightly to the idea that anyone would want to be around someone who has a Pinterest-worthy level of control and command of herself and her surroundings.

In truth, deep down I know the most welcoming spaces are those where someone is their messy authentic self. Shove the stuff on the seat to the floor and take this mug of coffee. Let's send the kids outside and chat. At work I'm drawn to the women who say "Here's how we thought we would do it ... but here's what happened ... looking for ideas on what to do next ... what do you think?"

I think even in this season of life I feel a little uncomfortable about officially being in "leadership." Yet I'm realizing it's more important to me to make room at tables and space for other people to be safe, rather than avoid the spotlight that will inevitably show all my messy bits. I want to muse about what kind of crazy we were experiencing. I want to laugh about what was going wrong because that was the only way through. That's what makes those gatherings fun and productive. Get past the performance and get to the ideas.

We haven't arrived yet. I can't say this process of inviting others into my Poop Years for an up-close look is solving all of my problems, but it is much less lonely. Being asked to weigh in on things—to talk about what I did to conceive of a process of aggregating data or getting people to participate in a program—is always exciting because I can hand off what I know and they can take it even further. Slowly, I am learning to let go.

I once heard a story about monkey traps. The trap had holes just big enough for a hand to pass through. On the other side of the wall was a banana or a treat. The chimps could get to the bananas, but if they closed their fists, they wouldn't be able to get the fruit through the hole. Rather than drop the fruit and get free, they were in a perpetual trap of their own doing.

Working and parenting with a rigid defensive mind is a lot like that—there is no reward for holding so tightly to perfection. In many ways, holding more loosely to those expectations and rolling with the changes brings rewards. Truly, it is in the vulnerability of knowing and allowing yourself to be seen in the mess that you are able to conceive of new ways to bend and adjust with whatever comes next. And unlike someone on a pedestal, there's no danger of falling; someone is right next to you to keep you company.

About the Author

*As a geographer, **Natalie Lee** blends her love of people with a fascination for place, finding fulfillment when relationships bring unlikely partners together to do meaningful work. With more than 20 years in geospatial technology, Natalie has held roles including Deputy Geospatial Information Officer for Georgia, Director on the National States Geographic Information Council Board, Program Manager for Georgia's 911 data program, and co-chair of the Family Support and Resources Committee at her children's school. Natalie lives in Atlanta's vibrant Kirkwood neighborhood, where she and her husband raise three rambunctious children and do their level best to keep the wheels on their ever-changing professional and family buses.*

your turn...

Embrace the imperfect

Have you ever found yourself getting defensive about a project or situation, either at work or at home? What do you think made you feel that way?

Do you sometimes hold yourself to a higher standard of perfection than you hold other people in your life? How does this impact your relationships and how you feel?

How does the idea of letting go of "perfect" sit with you? Does it feel like a cop out?

If you could reframe the idea of "perfect" to give yourself some leeway, what would that look like? How might you feel if you could let go ... even a little bit?

Write down your thoughts on the next few pages.

_____

_____

_____

_____

_____

_____

_____

_____

_____

_____

_____

_____

_____

_____

RULE 7

Walk Through the Door Anyway

by Susan Miller

Change is never neat. It's rarely welcome, and it's almost never on your terms.

I've carried a lesson from Pema Chödrön, an American-born Tibetan Buddhist nun and teacher, with me for most of my adult life. Her work focuses on helping people face change, fear, and uncertainty with compassion and grace. She teaches that when life falls apart, the bravest thing we can do is stay present with it —even when we want to run away. (Learn more at www.PemaChodronFoundation.org)

For me, that has always felt like standing in front of a door you don't want to open—because you know once you do, you'll never be the same again. The hardest part isn't walking through the door. It's deciding to.

For me, that door was my brother's death.

He wasn't just my big brother—he was my best friend, my person. When cancer ravaged his body, it came fast ... and for that, I'm grateful he did not suffer long. Tumors aggressively grew to fill his lungs, suffocating him to death over the course of three months and eight days. From the day he went to the doctor thinking he had a lingering cold, to the day he died, that's all the time we had.

I took leave from work and spent that time at his side. My mother and I cared for him—she during the day, me at night—because he was largely unable to sleep. The tumors were quickly filling his lungs, stealing the air he needed to breathe. If he drifted off for too long, he'd lose his fragile rhythm and his breathing would falter. So his body unkindly kept him awake.

As the days went on, he could no longer lie down; the pressure on his lungs made it impossible. Even when his body cried out for rest, he had to stay upright. When he started to slump, I'd gently lift him back into position, hoping each time that he might steal just one more minute of sleep.

On the day he died, when his lungs were too full to allow much movement at all, I climbed into his bed behind him. I slid my body into position to hold him upright, my legs wrapped around his hips, my chest against his back, my arms steadying him as he finally let go of holding himself up.

I whispered into his ear, over and over again: "It's okay to go. I love you."

When his body began to fail and his blood struggled to flow, his hands got cold first. As the effect moved up his arms, where my hands were wrapped around him, holding him steady, I could feel my own fingers sinking into his flesh as the circulation diminished.

His faint breaths grew further apart, until they stopped entirely.

I was numb. Unbelieving. The universe stood still and crashed down on me all at once.

The doctors couldn't pronounce him at first because their stethoscopes picked up my heartbeat through his chest. It wasn't until they made me crawl out from under him, as I collapsed to the floor, unable to stand, clutching his leg as if I could somehow tether him back, that they confirmed what I already knew.

I have regrets around his death, but holding him as he died is not one of them. That was the easiest decision I've ever made—and the most shattering. It split me wide open. Terror and love wrapped together.

What I do regret is trying so hard to stay "upbeat" for him during those months. The doctors were honest—it was bad—but there was still this implied fight we were supposed to have. So I outwardly stayed positive. I tried to carry enough optimism for all of us. I tried to make things feel possible, even as everything felt crushing.

In hindsight, I sometimes wonder if I should have spent more time making space for his grief, a lesson I carry in my leadership style now. I've learned that creating room for others to tell the truth about what they're carrying, even when it's painful, is one of the greatest gifts you can give. My brother couldn't even allow himself to cry the day the doctors told him there was no hope, that he would die soon. His breath was so fragile, so tenuous, that he didn't dare break the rhythm that was keeping him alive, even for a moment, to cry or scream.

A few days before he died, he told me he was tired. He said "no" to me for the first time during those three months, when I asked him to get up and walk a bit to help his full-body swelling. He just said, "No honey, I just can't."

It was such a simple sentence. But it was enormous.

In that moment, he was leading me. He was teaching me something I'll carry with me forever. Sometimes, you have to let go of the fight. Sometimes, you have to sit in the truth—even when it's brutal and your heart breaks into a million pieces you're certain will never come back together again.

I walked through that door because I loved him. And it shattered me. But still, I walked through.

You must walk through the door, even when it's the last thing you want to do. You must be present. You must show up.

Finding the courage to let go

After my brother's death, I thought a lot about how we handle loss—and the change, discomfort, and conflict that so often follow. Not just in life, but in leadership.

Again and again, I've found myself doing at work what I did at his bedside; trying to hold it all together for everyone else. Stay upbeat. Push forward. Keep fighting. Sometimes that's what's needed. But other times, it becomes a way to avoid the harder truth; that some change can't be fixed or managed. It can only be witnessed. And walked through.

The lesson I try to carry—and live—is this: Real leadership, whether for yourself or for others, doesn't mean pretending everything will be okay. It means making space to tell the truth about how hard it really is.

Some lessons must be learned over and over again, and letting go appears to be that kind of lesson for me. No matter how much I think I've learned it, life keeps offering me another chance to practice.

Several years after my brother's death, I faced another door. This one wasn't as painful as losing him, but in some ways it was harder to summon the courage to open.

Walking through death is something you do for love. Walking away from your career feels like failure.

On paper, it was my dream job. In reality, it had been eroding my spirit for years. I was managed by people who lacked vision, ruled through fear, or were driven by jealousy. And I was stubborn. I kept thinking surely I can fix this. Surely if I say the right thing or work the extra hours, or go the extra mile, I can turn it into the dream I wanted it to be.

But that's not how it works.

Eventually, I had to choose—quit, or lose myself entirely. So I walked away.

What followed was grief; a deep sense of loss. Not for what the job really was, but for what I had imagined it could be, and fought so hard to make real. It felt like mourning something I loved, even if that love was more about hope than reality. I've never been divorced, but I imagine it's something like that; grieving the life you wanted, not the one you actually had.

I loved the people I supported. I loved what the job could have been. But in the end, I had to grieve the dream—and the version of me who believed that trying harder would always be enough.

That experience, like my brother's death, reshaped me. It taught me that love and effort, no matter how deep or fierce, aren't always enough to save something. And that walking away doesn't mean you've failed.

Sometimes, it means you've finally learned to value yourself enough to stop carrying the burden of fixing something that was never yours to fix.

That job—and everything I went through during and after it—continues to shape the way I lead today. The team I managed then, and the ones that came after, I believe (and hope) have done well. Not because we had every resource we needed (we didn't) but because I've tried to give them the kind of support I never received and always longed for. I want to empower others to be their very best, not just at work but in life. It's more than a belief; it's how I try to move through the world. It's a core value I do my best to live every day—at work, at play, and everywhere in between.

It's uncomfortable to say that out loud. Not just because it might sound braggy or boastful, but because it means admitting that something went well because of me. Because I showed up a certain way. Because I worked to create the kind of environment I wish someone had created for me. There's this nagging voice in my head that chimes in: "Bragging about something immediately extinguishes its flame."

But here's the thing: I'm learning that staying silent about growth or success isn't always humility. Sometimes it's shrinking. And shrinking doesn't help the people I'm trying to support. So I'm practicing saying the quiet things out loud:

- that I care deeply.

- that I try really hard.

- that I am proud of what I've done.

- that I've learned a lot, and I'm still learning.

The irony is if anyone in my life—work or personal—refused to share their successes or celebrate their accomplishments, I'd be quite cross with them (in a supportive way, of course). Yet here I sit, thinking, "Yes, but that doesn't apply to me!" A learning moment, perhaps.

At the heart of it, I think of my brother. In those final weeks, I wanted nothing more than to hold him up and to give him rest. I didn't have that power, I couldn't take that weight away from him, but I can carry that lesson forward. I couldn't give him ease, but I can offer it to others now. And that's why, underneath everything else, my leadership will always be about creating spaces where people can breathe, tell the truth, and find their way through.

This shows up everywhere; in life, in love, and in leadership.

When I'm leading through change, I am tempted to protect others and shoulder the burden myself. I want to fight with optimism. I want to steer the boat, so others don't have to carry the weight, even when the current has other plans.

But I'm learning that sometimes the bravest thing you can do is stop paddling so hard and simply be in the moment as it is ... not as you wish it were.

Sometimes the greatest gift you can offer is space— the space for someone to name their fear, their exhaustion, their grief. I think often of my brother here. His breath was so fragile that he couldn't risk releasing his sorrow. Watching that taught me something I carry into leadership: how devastating it can be when there's no room to exhale.

Leadership isn't about holding it all together so no one else has to feel it; it's about creating space for people to breathe in and out with ease, even when the air feels thin. It's about letting them lay down what's heavy, even for a moment, and knowing someone will hold them up until they can find their rhythm again.

As I've gotten better at this, I've learned some valuable lessons:

- Sometimes you have to hold the people you love as they go.

- Sometimes you have to let your team tell you they're overwhelmed.

- Sometimes you have to say, "I don't know how this ends, but I'm here with you anyway."

That's love.

That's leadership.

That's life.

And still, you walk through the door. Even when it's terrifying. Even when it shatters your heart. Even when you don't know what's on the other side.

That's where the growth is. And when you arrive, bring all the grace and dignity you can muster—for yourself and for everyone else. You must show up!

That's where real leadership begins.

About the Author

Susan Miller is a leader and advocate for showing up to support her friends and colleagues. She has served in Geospatial Information Officer roles for more than two decades across both conservation and public service, guiding efforts at the intersection of people, data and decisions. Susan holds degrees in Conservation Science and Geospatial Science, and her leadership has been recognized nationally with honors such as the prestigious Esri President's Award and recognition as one of the nation's top geospatial leaders and top women in technology. Her story is shaped by loss, resilience, and the belief that creating safe and supportive work environments is essential to success. When she is not working, she enjoys time with family, friends, and her four-legged companions, and advocates for causes she is passionate about.

your turn...

Walk through the door anyway

One tool I'd love to share is what I call a Stinkin' Thinkin' session (also known as a "worst-case scenario" meeting). Before taking on something that makes you anxious—at work or in life—gather yourself and your team and name all the cataclysmic ways things could go wrong. Every possible pitfall, disaster, or fear gets said out loud. Nothing's off limits.

And this isn't just a tame risk assessment exercise; it's primal. Get creative. Go full apocalyptic if you have to. Then, imagine yourself in that terrifying space—in the absolute worst-case scenario(s)—and ask:

What does it really look like in here? How would this truly impact the project, or our team? What would/could we do to bring ourselves out of this place? Is it really that bad? Or are there ways out of here that prove we'll be fine?

This practice takes some of the power out of fear and uncertainty. It helps us name the scary thing out loud and then ask ourselves: "And now what? Is it really all that bad when we look it in the face and test the reality of the impact?"

It doesn't erase the inevitable scariness of change. But it does give you a way to walk through the door with eyes wide open, and with each other. It makes room for truth, reality, gut-checks, and the courage to sit side by side.

Think of a big change you're facing now, or one you've faced in the past. Big here means big to you—whether it might seem small or huge to someone else doesn't matter.

What's the absolute worst-case scenario you can imagine? If everything fell apart, how would it truly affect you, your work, or your relationships?

What resources, strengths, or people could help you navigate that moment?

What would "finding your way through" look like, even if it wasn't perfect?

Looking back from the other side, what might you learn or gain from having walked through it?

Use the space on the following pages to work through this "what if." Note the emotions that surface—and what they reveal about your fears, your resilience, and your capacity to keep going.

When you finish, take a step back and check in with yourself. Does the worst-case scenario feel as overwhelming as you first imagined, or do you see pathways through it you hadn't noticed before?

Often the simple act of exploring your fears shows you that many of them are more manageable than they seemed—and that your panic was never the full truth of the situation.

_____

_____

_____

_____

_____

_____

_____

_____

_____

_____

_____

_____

_____

_____

_____

RULE 8
Embrace the Uncertainty
by Kate Hickey

As humans, we all crave a sense of control over our environments. It's a survival instinct. We create constructs—both tangible and intangible—to reflect our values and view of the world, and to create structure, safety and meaning in our lives. When we face uncertainty, that sense of control evaporates, often triggering anxiety. Knowing what's coming allows us to prepare; not knowing feels like being vulnerable and powerless. It can feel like a leap into a vast, empty chasm. But that space—that "letting go"—is what can enable valuable change to take place.

I've always been a big visualizer. Before a trip to a new place, I imagine walking through the streets, feeling the blast of heat or chill on my skin, tasting the coffee. Researching and preparing and planning so I can take full advantage of this escape from my everyday life. Yet without a doubt, my favorite and most impactful travel experiences are those I've had when I went off script. When I let myself be fully in the moment, my senses on full alert, exhaling and immersing myself in something completely new and giving myself the space to see the world and myself differently.

When I was 23, I saved up my money from a post-college catering gig and booked a plane ticket to Southeast Asia. Other than my Lonely Planet guidebook with suggestions for inexpensive guest houses (essentially rooms for rent) and paper maps, I had no firm plans. I had no smartphone, no internet access, no Uber app, no Google Maps. (Now that I have kids approaching this age, I sympathize with what my mother must have endured in my absence!) I distinctly remember hugging my mother tightly at the airport then stepping away and rounding the corner into the international flight corridor. I was completely alone—more space than I had ever experienced and it simultaneously felt exhilarating and like I was in free fall. Two flights and many hours later, I landed in Ho Chi Minh City, drenched in heat and smells and foreign sounds. Just getting through the day's decisions and experiences to meet my basic needs took up so much energy and thought! Where will I sleep? How will I get from the bus station to my room? Even eating—I was so worried about WHAT I was eating, studying it for clues. What's really in this sauce? What is this vegetable? I remember the day I let go. I told myself, ALL these people around me are eating this mystery food and they're certainly fine. They aren't wasting all this energy trying to KNOW exactly what it is. So I ate my lunch and I was fine too. I look back on those few months as ones that shaped me in profound ways. I was in a suspended "leap of faith," caught midair, not knowing where I would land. It was in that gap I began to accept uncertainty and trust myself.

I'm a sucker for the reality survival series *Alone* (www.history.com/shows/alone) on the History Channel where participants compete equipped with minimal tools to outlast each other in a remote location in a challenge of self-reliance and endurance. Are the most successful ones the ones who painstakingly planned and strategized, or are the winners the ones who embraced uncertainty and remained agile? Does their vision of what success looks like blind them to the unplanned path to actual success?

By remaining unattached to a particular vision, the "flexible" players can assess their resources, their surroundings, and their situation objectively, and adjust quickly to who they need to be and what they need to do to survive. I have thought many times of a woman named Theresa on the show who built a subterranean pit house for her shelter. It was brilliantly planned but took enormous amounts of energy to construct; ultimately she was forced to concede defeat as she wasted away in front of the cameras. I was rooting for her and wondered many times whether she could have won had she pivoted her energy away from the elaborate structure and toward hunting or gathering more food. She held on so tightly to the certainty of her winning plan—that predefined vision of herself—that she couldn't acknowledge she was starving to death.

There is joy and growth and liberation in letting the "best path" reveal itself, letting go of the preconceived visions in our heads. Yet in our achievement-oriented, "check the box" culture, we are so driven toward reaching a predefined goal that it becomes all too easy to lose our openness and receptivity to change. Somewhere between over-planning and total whimsy is the space we need to see a new way forward; and uncertainty is that space where true change becomes possible.

The problem with efficiency

As those who know me will attest, I am someone who seeks efficiency. I focus on operations at work, searching out the work that can be repeated and made more efficient, and always looking for ways to shave hours or even simply minutes off processes. At home, I'm the queen of the speed clean, the simple dinner and never touching the mail more than once. I make quick decisions in the interest of moving on.

As an adult, there is so much emphasis on efficiency. We are so stretched for time, we naturally want to shave time from every task. Cooking. Cleaning. Eating. Exercising. Communicating. Traveling. We measure and track and chart it all. We collect data on our sleeping, our caloric intake, our steps. At work, we track how many minutes it takes to complete a technical task or write a proposal. We seek tools to automate and streamline. And believe me, I recognize there is tremendous value in efficiency! Yet what does this quest for efficiency do to our life experience?

To be truly effective, efficiency relies on repetition and certainty. Throw a few unknowns into the mix and suddenly the perfected workflow breaks down. Removing uncertainty keeps the gears running smoothly, yes, but is that what we want out of life?

Repetitive and routine days filled with familiar experiences actually pass more quickly, according to our brains (Skylark & Gheorghui, 2017). In a repetitive routine the brain doesn't find much that's new, interesting, or worth storing, so less memory encoding is going on. With less memories being encoded, there's less to look back on, and the days pass largely unnoted by our brains.

These were likely those "efficient" days where we took the shortest route to work, met with familiar colleagues, and cooked a meal we've made a thousand times. Our brains were on auto pilot and not fully engaged. Contrast this with unusual or novel days—when we travel to new places, experience unexpected events or rich sensory experiences, talk with interesting new people—these are the days our brains create a rich series of memories, making time move slower in the moment and the day feel longer in hindsight.

I need to remind myself that efficiency is not the ultimate end goal—that is so hard to do! I need to remember to measure the quality of my days, seeking out and embracing those rich sensory experiences. These could be small doses of uncertainty where we try a new food or wander a new neighborhood in our city, or perhaps big ways like taking on a new role or job with completely new people, processes, responsibilities. Our brains fully engage with the new challenges, without knowing exactly what's next. We feel … more alive.

But what about when the "space" opens up unexpectedly?

Seeking out change and uncertainty has huge benefits. What if we did not choose to introduce uncertainty? What if we're hiking a path, and the path just simply ends? No trail marker. No worn path in the dirt or trampled grass hinting at the way to go. When uncertain events disrupt our plans or beliefs, they can shake our sense of identity and purpose.

Since moving from California to Boston in 1997, I have become intrigued by marathon runners. I remember watching my first Boston Marathon, curbside in the Coolidge Corner neighborhood of Brookline. Thirty-thousand runners from dozens of countries passed by with surprising diversity in size and shape. They shared a common experience that day, as their participation in the race was a culmination of their discipline and planning. Training for the marathon had become their sense of purpose and direction for months —maybe even years—on full display for all to see and celebrate. These runners had trained and prepared for thousands of hours and thought about all the details, down to which shoelaces they would wear, what they would eat for breakfast, and their precise pacing. They embraced the ideas that with discipline comes certainty, and with certainty comes success.

While I was not a spectator at the Marathon in 2013, I have imagined the experience of the runners that fateful day when a senseless act of terror shattered the event. The Boston Marathon bomb killed three people and robbed a dozen others of their limbs. Hundreds were physically injured and thousands were, without a doubt, psychologically traumatized. The juxtaposition of goodwill and unity against the brazen violence of the moment was heartbreaking; the war-zone footage of violence on streets so familiar to me was rattling. While the images focused on the site of the bombing near the finish lines, I've often thought about the runners who were miles back, completely unaware of what had just occurred. One moment they were focusing on the smiles in the crowd and the next, their focus was obliterated as they were told to STOP. Their focus was obliterated, their identities suddenly changed as they realized, "I cannot continue on this path—I will not succeed today. I will not achieve my vision."

Adrianne Haslet was one of the bombing survivors; she lost her left leg below the knee that day. Adrianne had been a professional ballroom dancer and was standing near the finish line as a spectator when the bombs exploded. Despite the trauma, Adrianne turned her recovery into a story of resilience and acceptance of change (https://www.youtube.com/watch?v=giDxtf0i850). Just 200 days after the bombing, she danced on stage again using a prosthetic limb and later she was featured on Dancing with the Stars. In 2016, she ran the Boston Marathon using a specially designed prosthetic for running. She didn't just recover physically—she redefined her identity and embraced a new path.

Oh, the things we fear! They punch us in the gut and shake our sense of identity to its core. You will not go to your dream college. You did not get the promotion. You will not be a mother. You did not succeed. Punch, punch, punch.

So we protect ourselves with certainty. We build elaborate scaffolding around our lives to ensure things go according to plan. We establish routine and try as hard as we can to remove the unknowns. Can we reframe uncertainty, whether chosen by us or not, as possibility?

What if we reframe our thinking? What if instead of "with enough planning and preparation I can eliminate the unknowns," we tell ourselves "I am resourceful and flexible and can adjust to the situation as it evolves"?

Instead of "my vision or dream is now shattered and will never come true" we say "I now have the space to let new experiences in—ones that I never had the room to imagine previously."

Instead of "How can I guarantee this outcome" we ask "what step can I take today" to move in the right direction.

Instead of imagining all the possible terrible things that can go wrong, what happens if we stay present and in the moment? This is what I know now. Yes, this path is foggy ... yet I can see the next step in front of me. The key to managing uncertainty is to take action without needing absolute clarity—to walk the foggy path a step at a time, staying present and creating new answers as we go.

About the Author

Kate Hickey *is the Chief Operating Officer for Sanborn Geospatial, helping teams across the company navigate technological, organizational, and cultural change. She loves listening to podcasts, planning trips to new places, and soaking in any time her teenagers will offer. She lives north of Boston with her husband and two children.*

your turn...

Know your why

What uncertainties are you facing in your life right now? What's your level of comfort with not knowing the outcome or future?

Do you have the resources and flexibility you need to face these uncertainties? If not, what do you feel you lack?

Instead of "my vision or dream is now shattered and will never come true" can you say "I now have the space to let new experiences in— ones that I never had the room to imagine previously" and be willing to explore a different outcome?

How can you break down "what's next" into small, doable steps so you can make some progress and stay present in the moment? Use the space on the following pages to write down your thoughts.

_____

_____

_____

_____

_____

_____

_____

_____

_____

_____

_____

_____

_____

_____

RULE 9

Be Uniquely You
by Lindsey Peña, PhD

Dream Big Dreams

You have to dream big dreams if you want to go real far;
You have to plan your way if you want to make
the most of your day.
It's the little steps you take that add up to form a
line, It's the completion of small deeds over a
given set of time.
One day is not enough
but sometimes it's all you've got;
So do what you can do with everything you've got.
Once you remove the clutter, it's easier for you to
see the path of your purpose, truth, and clarity.

We're here for only a short time,

and then we are gone;
Leaving behind our imprints in our own life's
marathon.

You may not be the fastest or even look the part.
You may not know the way or even where to start.
But it's up to you to put on your shoes and tie up
your laces to start determining the specifics of
your destined races.

Little by little, day by day
the path becomes clear, showing the way.
It's not about perfection, the prize, or even the
finish. And sometimes the path will become
unclear and even hard to distinguish.

Uniqueness is the key,
and it's found in you and me.
It's up to you to bring your true self out;
that is what this journey is all about.

Let's take a moment and talk about something extraordinary. Something so unique, so bold, so completely irreplaceable ... You.

If you don't think you are unique, I want you to consider this—I once saw a LinkedIn post from Ancestry.com about how many ancestors it took going back multiple generations to create the one-and-only you:

Parents: 2
Grandparents: 4
Great-Grand Parents: 8
2nd Great-Grand Parents: 16
3rd Great-Grand Parents: 32
4th Great-Grand Parents: 64
5th Great-Grand Parents: 128
6th Great-Grand Parents: 256
7th Great-Grand Parents: 512
8th Great-Grand Parents: 1,024
9th Great-Grand Parents: 2,048
10th Great-Grand Parents: 4,096

...and the list keeps growing.

Thousands of people made choices, overcame challenges, and lived lives that ultimately led to the moment of your existence. Your life is a once-in-history opportunity to contribute your unique self to the world.

For much of my life, I thought I had to fit a mold. I held back. I played it safe. Then something shifted when I turned 40, just as the whole world locked down for Covid in 2020. Maybe it was the '90s-style buzz undercut I gave myself that I'd always wanted but could never muster the courage earlier. Then again, maybe it was the silence of quarantine that made me realize I had spent way too long trying to be "normal." Up until this point, I had been hiding, shape-shifting into versions of myself I thought the world expected me to be.

I was wrong. It's not what others think of you that matters. What truly matters is what you think of yourself. It's okay to do things differently. It's okay to stand out. It's okay to hone your uniqueness and show your true authentic self to the world. I found an incredible freedom when I stopped trying to be like someone else, fill someone else's expectations, took the outside pressures off, and finally embraced that I am enough, just as is.

So, what makes you ... you? Whatever it is, own it.

Our unique stories are our strengths. Whether you like it or not, the biggest constant throughout your entire life will be you. You'll always be there, no matter the situation or circumstance. There is just no escaping yourself. In fact, the longest relationship you will ever experience is your relationship with yourself. That's good news, because it means you have the choice to be whoever you want to be ... and you have the power to write your own story. I learned the only real limitation holding me back was my own mind. And I suspect I'm not alone in that.

We all tell ourselves internal stories ... yet are these stories actually rooted in reality? Are they helpful? Are they even ours? Think about what is real versus what is not. What label or meaning have you attached to the stories of your life? Are they valid? Are they skewed? Or perhaps, is there another interpretation?

Defining Moments

Some stories shake us more than they shape us. It's a lighthearted joke now when I tell people that my sister is the literal rocket scientist, where alas, I am just the lowly PhD. I joke now, but as a kid growing up it took me years to realize that I had my own value and worth not tied to any self-imposed comparisons.

I was the baby in my family. Not only was I the youngest child, I was also raised by first borns; both my mother and father were first borns in their respective families growing up. In my childhood eyes, it seemed my older sister, Jennifer, was the perfect child, especially to my parents and other adults. She could do no wrong.

The striking physical differences between the two of us helped to solidify those beliefs. She had straight, long hair compared to my kinky, curly hair; she had a thin frame compared to my curves; and she embodied my ideals of maturity and intelligence. She was four years my senior, and I was always referred to as "Jennifer's little sister" by my teachers. She had left some large, amazing academic shoes I thought would never be able to fit into, much less outgrow.

It also didn't help that I grew up in the "sight word" generation method of education. In early reading fundamentals, some schools teach phonics—the ability to sound out letters to be able to decode words; some schools teach reading by the sight word method, memorizing words by the way that they look; and some schools teach a blend of both methods, which in my opinion, is the best of both worlds.

As a sight word child, I might comprehend the word, I might have heard the word spoken before, I might have even used the word in my own vocabulary, but if I had never seen the word written down before and I was trying to read it, I would have no clue how to say the word and would most likely embarrass myself and say the word wrong.

Because of this, I hated reading out loud. I was one of those students, trying to look really busy, nose down in my text book when the teacher would ask for volunteers. I would secretly be praying, please don't pick me, please don't pick me.

I have vivid memories of being in my 5th grade classroom during a history lesson where the teacher was having each student in the class read a portion of an assignment out loud. Feverishly, I would try to count the number of students ahead of me and rapidly scan the text and try to figure out where I was going to have to read. I would then proceed to read the three or four sentences over and over and over again so I would not make a mistake and sound stupid and silly in front of the rest of my classmates.

Lacking a strong basis in reading ate away at my self-confidence. Combined with the self-imposed high standard perception I had bestowed on my sister, I felt I could never measure up. I felt stupid. I felt worthless. So, I gave up. I settled. I figured that I shouldn't even try, because, why bother? I bought into a false story that I was "the fun one," "the social butterfly," "the life of the party," but could never be the "smart one."

What I did not know or recognize as a child was that my sister worked incredibly hard for her grades. She would spend hours working on her school work. In my mind, everything came naturally and easily to her. While I still managed to maintain decent grades while not trying or putting in any real effort in my early school years, I often wonder what might have been if I had actually applied myself. What could I have achieved if I stopped comparing myself to the false version of my sister I had created in my own mind? This story I bought into—that I would never compare, never be as capable, and never be like my perfect older sister—had a strong hold on my young life.

I carried that story for years, until adulthood when I lived with my sister for a year. As I began to spend in-depth adult time with my sister, I realized the story I had been telling myself all those years was flawed. A defining moment for me was when she told me she always thought I was more naturally academically astute than her because I was able to achieve decent grades without much effort. My story was flawed. The narrative I'd internalized all my life wasn't true. I had never seen the hours she spent studying behind closed doors, just like she had never known the pressures I had placed on myself trying to measure up to her before I finally gave up.

Sometimes a fresh perspective is all it takes.

From there, I began to change my narrative. I began to question what made other people's thoughts, opinions and ideas carry more weight than my own. Why was it that I didn't feel smart or capable until my sister told me her opinion of me when, in reality, the only opinion that should matter most and carry the most weight should be my own? This breakthrough allowed me to find myself again and rewrite the old flawed version of myself.

You don't need to reinvent yourself. You need to recognize yourself.

Change is nothing new. It's nothing you haven't already experienced or gone through before. Sometimes we initiate the change and sometimes change just shows up unannounced. Fight it, resist it, deal with it or welcome it, change can be very emotionally charged. But it is also important to put some rational reasoning, intention, and thoughtful planning behind the emotion.

Let's change and reframe our approach to how we think about ourselves to better navigate change.

In challenging situations or times of change, it's important to remember you're never truly starting over. Your slate hasn't been wiped clean. You have more knowledge than you realize. Take some time for self-reflection and really get to know yourself, your strengths and your positive character traits.

"Take a moment to slow down. Settle into where you are right now. We are all here for a different reason. Chasing different goals, different missions. Whatever it is that you are striving for, whatever it is that you desire ... you are worthy. You are capable. You are powerful. And you will be successful. You already are successful."

Katie Grillo, Women in GIS (WiGIS) NE Founder & Cochair

Think of your skills and experiences as tools in your toolbox. You've got more than you think. You're building on everything you've learned and those experiences are all part of what makes you special and capable. Don't ever discount your own personal skills and experiences. Once you have learned a skill, it will be with you forever. You can have everything else taken away—your money, material objects, jobs, friends, and networks, but what you have learned and how it has shaped you and developed you is untouchable. The knowledge you have, and how you've changed as you've learned, will stay with you forever.

What have you done in the past that you can build from? How can your knowledge and skills be repurposed? Look back at your past projects, skills, and knowledge. How can you use them again or tweak them for something new? Your past is full of resources; you just have to recognise them and tap into their power.

The Montessori Moment

I once had the experience of being able to sit in a Montessori classroom. Organized chaos is the word I would use to describe it … and markedly different from the structured, formal public education classrooms I am most familiar with—both attending and teaching. It was interesting how the classroom was set up with different stations with various projects available to the students. There were no assigned activities and there wasn't any traditional classroom-type instruction done by the teacher. No beginning signals that class was starting like roll call, talking about the date, or reviewing the schedule for the day. Instead, the children drifted in and chose their activities, led only by curiosity. One boy, probably around five years of age, migrated towards a water basin. He filled it with water and then found a quiet place near some tables, put on a blue smock, found a bar of soap and scrub brush. Tools in hand, he began scrubbing down one of the tables. Perhaps he had a family member who cleaned houses or businesses for a living, or maybe he had a natural tendency to clean. The Montessori environment intrigued me. Here is a situation in which children could ultimately express their true talents and interests in an open and non-restrained environment. They could do—or not do—as they pleased.

In that classroom, with no assigned seating and no rigid schedule, children could simply be. They needed no one's permission to choose their path. The experience stayed with me, and I applied that to my own life. We don't need permission to be ourselves. I just need the freedom to explore who we really are.

So I ask you this: are you going to let your most unique self come out and play today? And let that unique you help you manage the changes you are going through?

You are the Mosaic

Being uniquely you is your competitive edge and it's your cumulative lived experiences that create the most authentic version of you. You're not just one identity either; rather you're the sum of your whole life of experiences. From awkward childhood experiences to career shifts to unexpected life lessons, every pixel of your life adds up to a one-of-a-kind image that no one else can replicate.

What if you could see yourself as a photo mosaic masterpiece? Photo mosaics are made of images composed of many smaller photos arranged in a specific way so that, when viewed from a distance, they form a larger, cohesive image. Each tiny photo usually relates in some way to the overarching image, making it visually and conceptually compelling. All of your seemingly unrelated experiences, skills, odd jobs, dreams and quirks are like those little photos. Individually, they're specific, but when you put them all together they combine to form one amazing, unique picture: YOU.

Sometimes, if you are too close to the nitty-gritty day-in, day-out circumstances in your life you can lose the perspective of the larger impact being made. So take a step back once in a while to see the full picture.

Change can be scary, but it can also be powerful. Growth happens in the "between" spaces—between certainty and risk, between planning and action, between the story you've lived and the one you're about to write.

Let's change and reframe our approach and how we think about ourselves to better navigate change. Because change will come and we can fight it, resist it, deal with it or welcome it. From ripples to waves, embrace all your life lessons and lean into your growth. Because one day at a time, step by step, you're creating something extraordinary.

So today, I challenge you. Ride the wave of inspiration. Say the thing. Take the step. Be you, fully and unapologetically. Because the world doesn't need a copy of someone else. It needs you. Fully. Fiercely. Boldly. Uniquely. YOU.

About the Author

Lindsey Peña, MBA, MPhil, PhD *is a seasoned nonprofit executive and organizational strategist whose career spans two decades of impact leading mission-driven initiatives across social services, education, and, most recently, the geospatial community. She currently serves as Chief Operating Officer of the National Geospatial Collaborative (NGC) and the National States Geographic Information Council (NSGIC). She holds a PhD in Management with a focus on Leadership and Organizational Change, a Master's in Philosophy in Management from Walden University, and an MBA in Strategy and Management from Western Governors University. In addition to her professional accomplishments, Lindsey is a lifelong learner and deeply committed to living and leading with authenticity. Residing in Tomball, Texas, outside of work she finds joy in supporting her daughter's latest adventures, capturing everyday moments through photography, and building meaningful connections wherever she goes.*

your turn...

Be uniquely you

What have you done in the past that you can build on when faced with change? How can your knowledge and skills be repurposed to fit your current circumstance?

Look back at your past projects, skills, and knowledge. How can you use them again or reinvent them to help you build something new?

What are the things that make you ... you? What lights you up and sparks your joy? How can you lean on these things to help you navigate change?

Write down your thoughts on the next few pages.

RULE 10
Find Your Joy
by Karen Rogers

Change.

Paradoxically, the only thing constant is change. Having lived through many significant life changes— some of my choosing and others that were imposed on me—I embraced this as my life motto decades ago.

It's not a new phrase; I'm sure you've heard some version of it ... but what does it really mean? Change truly is inevitable. Nothing remains static in this life. Whether the changes we go through are self-directed or not our choice, we all need some strategies to get through them. One strategy that has helped me get through the dark times is to always look for my joy.

I started writing this chapter in early 2025, a time of huge uncertainty and flux for many. As a federal employee, I knew by February I needed something to be excited about, something to spark my joy again and regain even a little bit of control. While out running my errands one weekend, I was at Menards and it hit me—tomatoes!

I have always been a big gardener, but it has been many years since I've been able to grow a decent plot. I absolutely love nurturing things—green things in particular, although I've done a pretty decent job with my human children. Somehow in the years when my kids were young, I found the time to start my garden from seeds, starting my tomatoes inside while snow still blanketed the ground.

Seeing those tiny green seedlings on a warming mat while it's still cold outside nurtures hope in me. Those little shoots remind me that life continues on its perpetual cycle. So on that cold February Sunday, when I knew I needed something better than doom scrolling to fill my evenings, I bought three packets of tomato seeds —red, orange, and yellow cherry varieties.

When I got home I rooted through the shed to dig out the warming mat and seed starting tray. Every day since then I got to check in on my tomatoes. I talked to them about how they're growing and when they're going to be re-potted or transplanted outside. Now that they're outside, I tell them about the weather or compliment their growing blossoms. I love watching them transform from tiny seeds to plants over five feet tall covered in fruit. It's so gratifying to be the instigator of that change, especially while unwelcome and often scary change continues to crash around me. In a tangible way, caring for my tomatoes grounds me and brings me joy.

Taking those few moments out of my busy and stressful life (I'm a single mom with a demanding professional career) to find my joy is golden. No matter how bad my day might have been, when I see my tomatoes I smile. My reality is re-focused on a tangible object, thanks to my own agency over how I spend my time and attention, and suddenly the chaos around me is immaterial. The clock stops while I immerse myself in my joy. It is extremely therapeutic and rejuvenating. In this case, the change I am struggling to cope with is out of my control, but by taking time to find my joy each day, I am taking control of my attitude in the face of imposed and unknown changes.

On the other hand, sometimes we must choose to make a change in our lives. Thirteen years ago, I found myself in an emotionally abusive marriage, and the circumstances hit a boiling point. I had to get myself and my kids, ages 3 and 6, out in a hurry. On the drive back to the town I grew up in, heading to a safe place where I had lots of family to help us start over, I knew in my heart this would be a permanent move. In a matter of days, I went from being a stay-at-home wife and mom to being a single mom with two kids, no job, no house, and no money. Everything about my life had changed. Yet somehow, amidst raising two smart and energetic kids, landing a new professional job, arranging daycare, paying my bills, and figuring out who I was in this terrifying new landscape, I still found my joy in those moments I intentionally carved out for myself.

I learned the value of finding my joy from a young age. When I was barely 18 I started my career as a martial artist one week after high school graduation. I currently hold a 3rd Degree Black Belt in Hawaiian Kenpo and a 5th Degree Black Belt in Okinawan Kempo.

Before my marriage fell apart, I taught karate and tai chi classes in Pinedale, the tiny town I lived in for 15 years. Martial arts is something I know I am good at; continuing my training and sharing the practice with others brings me much joy. My favorite practice is *kata*, which are individual patterns that mimic fight scenes with multiple opponents.

Even in the early years of starting my life over, I would religiously get up at 5 or 5:30 in the morning to do my *kata* workout in the exercise room in my basement. The *kata* served not only as great physical exercise, but also provided a release of the intense mental stress and emotional tumult I was going through at the time. I can't tell you how therapeutic it feels to visualize taking down the people in your life who have wronged you ... and bonus points for taking out my anger in a safe and positive way. Doing my *kata* demanded discipline and dedication on my part, and to my credit I was making time to find my joy, while actively helping myself cope with change in real time.

Joy is one of those parts of life that is intensely personal, and it can definitely change as we grow and evolve. Maybe we've outgrown the specific things that used to bring us joy ... yet our capacity for that feeling remains. To me, finding joy is a constant in itself ... and sometimes it truly is the simplest thing ... the tomato growing in winter's dark days ... that brings the spark.

So now I encourage you to ask yourself what it is that brings you joy. Is it a big event you need to save up money for? Or maybe it's something you can develop from daily practice, or something completely new and creative you've always wanted to try. Whatever it is, work it into your life. Start small, start slow, try out different things until you find that spark. What cracks a smile on your face and lightens your load, if only for a moment. Find that thing and welcome it into your life.

About the Author

Karen Rogers, *aka the Geospatial Virtuoso of Wyoming, is a fifth-generation Wyomingite whose love of wide-open spaces led her from archaeology to a distinguished career in geospatial technology. She has served in leadership roles with the National States Geographic Information Council (NSGIC) and the Wyoming Geospatial Organization, and today is the Geospatial Program Manager for the Bureau of Land Management's Wyoming State Office. When not advancing the geospatial field, Karen enjoys gardening, skiing, backpacking, and martial arts.*

your turn...

Find your joy

When times are tough and you're feeling despair, what brings a spark of joy or makes you smile?

What could you see or do that would bring a smile to your face, create some warmth in your heart as part of your daily routine?

It can be any little thing—or a big thing if you have the means. Whatever it is, incorporate it into your life daily. Make a commitment to yourself to stop the clock to find your joy every day.

Write down your thoughts on the journaling pages that follow.

_____

_____

_____

_____

_____

_____

_____

_____

_____

_____

_____

_____

_____

_____

_____

_____

_____

_____

_____

_____

_____

_____

_____

_____

_____

_____

_____

_____

_____

_____

_____

ACKNOWLEDGEMENTS

This book would not have been possible without the commitment and hard work of each one of the 10 contributing authors. Jenna, Angela, Shea, Megan, Erin, Natalie, Susan, Kate, Lindsey, and Karen—your willingness to dig deeply and authentically share your personal stories was breathtaking. I watched in awe as you all encouraged each other and worked together brilliantly to create this book, *with the sole mission of helping others*. Special kudos to Jenna, Kate and Erin for serving as the Editorial Board and making sure this book actually made it into print. You're all rockstars.

I am profoundly grateful to have met each one of you through this project. You've made me laugh, cry and grow with your stories and I will always treasure this experience.

A special note of thanks goes to Frank Winters, for helping spark this collaboration *and* being there through it all as our number one fan. Your support means everything. And to John, for making sure I eat lunch ... and so many other reasons.

Carol Pearson
Founder & Publisher, Little Rules Publishing

End Notes

Winters, Frank. (2024). "10 Little Rules for Sharing Your Story." Little Rules Publishing.

Anderson-Lopez, K; and Lopez, R. *The Next Right Thing* [Song]. On the soundtrack of *Frozen 2* [Film]. Walt Disney Animation Studios.

Qian, S. (2020). *A Statistical Analysis of the Challenger Disaster.* RebellionResearch. https://blog.rebellionresearch.com/blog/a-statistical-analysis-of-the-challenger-accident

Krakauer, Jon. (1996). "Into the Wild." Villard.

Gupta, Sangana. (2025). *How a simple 4-box method can help you stress less and get more done.* Very Well Mind. https://www.verywellmind.com/how-the-eisenhower-matrix-helps-you-stress-less-11819774

Romney, C., Arroyo, A., Robles, T., and Zawadski, M. (2023). Hugs and Cortisol Awakening Response the Next Day: An Ecological Momentary Assessment Study. *International Journal of Environmental Research and Public Health.* 20(7).

Hu, Charlotte. (2024). *Why writing by hand is better for memory and learning.* Scientific American. https://www.scientificamerican.com/article/why-writing-by-hand-is-better-for-memory-and-learning/

Barry, K., Den Houter, K., and Guggenheim, K. (2024). *More Than a Program; a Culture of Women's Wellbeing at Work.* Gallup. https://www.gallup.com/workplace/653843/program-culture-women-wellbeing-work.aspx

Fry, R., Aragão, C., Hurst, K., and Parker, K. (2023). *In a Growing Share of U.S. Marriages, Husbands and Wives Earn About the Same.* Pew Research Center. https://www.pewresearch.org/social-trends/2023/04/13/in-a-growing-share-of-u-s-marriages-husbands-and-wives-earn-about-the-same

Skylark, William & Gheorghiu, Ana. (2017). Further Evidence That the Effects of Repetition on Subjective Time Depend on Repetition Probability. *Frontiers in Psychology.* 8. 1915.

CBS Evening News. (April 17, 2023). Boston Marathon bombing survivor shares her story. [video] https://www.youtube.com/watch?v=giDxtf0i850

your turn, your rules...

Use these blank pages to explore your thoughts around change ... and thank you for joining us on this journey with the Women of Geospatial Leadership!

_____

_____

_____

_____

_____

_____

_____

_____

_____

_____

_____

_____

_____

_____

_____

_____

_____

_____

_____

_____

_____

_____

_____

_____

_____

_____

_____

_____

_____

_____

A good review means the world to our authors.

If you enjoyed this book,
please leave a review on Amazon or Goodreads.

And thank you for supporting indie publishing at 10 Little Rules. Learn more about us at
www.10littlerules.com